TRUE
DESERT
ADVENTURES

First published in 2002 by Usborne Publishing Ltd,
Usborne House, 83-85 Saffron Hill,
London EC1N 8RT, England.
www.usborne.com

A catalogue record for this title is available
from the British Library.

ISBN 07945 03810

Printed in Great Britain

Designed by Brian Voakes
Illustrated by John Woodcock
Series Editors: Jane Chisholm and Rosie Dickins
Series designer: Mary Cartwright
Cover photograph © Jonathan Blair/CORBIS

These stories are based on a wide variety of sources and
historical documents, but the author is particularly indebted to
four writers without whose accounts this version would not
have been possible. These are Ralph Barker for *Verdict on a
Lost Flyer*, the story of Bill Lancaster; Charles Gallenkamp
for *Dragon Hunter*, a biography of Roy Chapman Andrews;
Annette Kobak for *Isabelle*, a biography of Isabelle Eberhardt;
and Henno Martin for *The Sheltering Desert*, his own
account of life in the Namib Desert.

TRUE
DESERT
ADVENTURES

Gill Harvey

CONTENTS

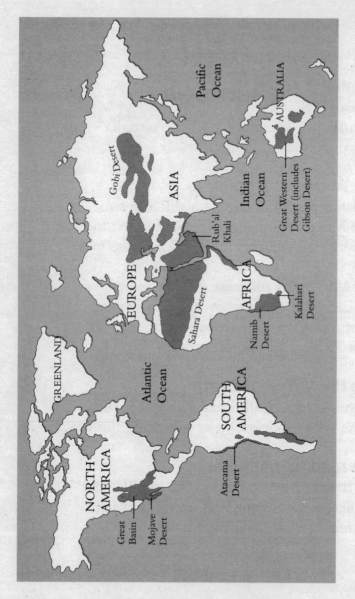

This map shows the main deserts of the world (marked by the dark shaded areas).

Life and death in the desert

Deserts are dangerous places. Wild and inhospitable, their extreme temperatures push human endurance to its limits, while their endless sand dunes and rocky plains make it incredibly difficult to navigate. But the greatest danger they pose is this: they are the driest places on earth. They suck water out of everything like a dry, hungry sponge. A desert is an area where less than 10cm (4 inches) of rain falls each year. That's very little indeed – so little that only the toughest, most specialized plants and animals can survive. So for humans, not only is there nothing to drink, but there's very little to eat, too.

It's true some groups of people have made the deserts their home, and have developed the necessary skills to survive. In the Sahara and Arabian Deserts, tribes of nomads lead a footloose lifestyle with their flocks of hardy sheep and goats, constantly on the move to find enough to live on. They know all the oases and wells, and can find their way even when the wind shifts the patterns of the dunes. But they've been doing this for thousands of years. Everyone else would really do much better to stay away...

Deserts take up a fifth of the world's land surface. The biggest of them all, the Sahara, covers a third of

Africa – an area roughly the size of the United States. It is also one of the hottest places on earth, with temperatures soaring as high as 58°C (136°F). The record for the driest place, though, goes to the Atacama Desert, in Chile, which can go for years without getting any rain at all.

Deserts are more varied than you might think; they're not all sandy and they're not all scorchingly hot. The Gobi Desert in Asia, for example, is classified as a 'cold desert'. Although it's hot in summer, in winter temperatures drop dramatically to well below freezing, bringing icy winds and even snow.

Despite the dangers, deserts still hold a romantic fascination, and people have ventured into them time and time again, often relatively unprepared. Deserts may be stunningly beautiful, but the attraction is more than that. Until recently, they were among the last great challenges for the adventurer, the last places on earth to be explored and mapped.

The stories in this book are about people who, for a variety of reasons, risked their lives in the world's driest places. For them, the desert may have been a challenge, a place that holds hidden secrets, or simply an obstacle to be crossed. Their adventures began when they stepped out of their own world, into the unknown. Their tales are of hardship, thirst and desperation, mixed with wonder and discovery. But, above all, they show that the perils of the desert have to be taken seriously. A harsh fate awaits anyone who dares to think otherwise...

Two men
and a dog

The world, it seemed, was going crazy. It was 1940, just after the outbreak of the Second World War, and the German army was marching across Europe. Far away in Africa, two Germans, Henno Martin and Hermann Korn, listened to the news on their radio with growing horror. The war's long tentacles could be felt even in Windhoek, the capital of Namibia, where they lived. Germans were being rounded up, in case they were Nazis, and were being locked away in internment camps. Their turn would come soon...

They sat on their porch one evening, thinking hard. They were geologists, and wanted nothing to do with a bloody, senseless war. They didn't like the idea of being locked up just because they were German, either.

"You know what we could do," said Hermann in a low voice.

"What?" asked Henno curiously.

"We always said that if a war came, we'd hide in the desert."

Henno stared at him. It was true – they had said that once, as a joke. But could they really do it? They had no idea how long the war would last. It might go on for years.

"What about Otto?" asked Henno.

"Otto?" Hermann looked at their dog, who was gazing at them, as always, with wagging tail and shining eyes. "We'll take him with us, of course."

On all their trips into the desert, Otto had been their faithful companion. There was no reason to change that now. Quickly, they made up their minds. They would load up their truck – and go. The Namib Desert offered plenty of places to hide. They would trust their luck to the wilds, until the war was over.

In four days, they had gathered together everything they needed. They could take basic foodstuffs with them – dried and canned food, tea, coffee, sugar and jam. To these they added a few luxuries such as chocolate and brandy. They took some kitchen equipment – sharp knives and a frying pan. They needed sleeping bags, a tarpaulin, and a few clothes; they added sewing equipment and a first aid kit. For the truck, they needed plenty of fuel, spare parts and tools. What else?

"My violin," said Hermann firmly. "I'm not leaving that behind."

Most important of all, however, was their radio and their guns. The radio would give them essential news of the outside world, and the progress of the war. It would run on the truck's battery, and let them know when it was safe to emerge from the desert. The guns were their lifeline. Their stores of food would have to be carefully rationed, and wouldn't be enough to live on. If they were going to survive, they would have to hunt. Rifles would have been best for hunting, but all rifles had been confiscated at the beginning of the war. They had only a shotgun and a pistol – not ideal, but these would have to do.

With the truck loaded, they set off along a route they knew would be difficult to trace. Not many white people knew the desert as well as they did. They set course for a secret canyon in the heart of the Namib Desert.

The Namib Desert stretches down the western edge of Namibia, a long strip of land that borders on the sea. The northern section of this coast is known as the Skeleton Coast. It is named after the victims of shipwrecks in the past – those who were lucky enough to reach the shore found no water or food to keep them alive; they would simply die in the merciless desert.

Part of the desert consists of some of the most spectacular sand dunes in the world, which rise and fall in shades of deep rust and orange. These offered little shelter or life for the two runaways, but there are other areas where the desert is rocky and rutted with deep canyons. Here, there are waterholes – and where there is water, there is life.

Taking a treacherous route with their truck, Henno and Hermann made their way to the top of the Kuisib canyon. Here, they stopped and surveyed the view – a wild, desolate landscape of jutting rocks and deep gorges, sheer cliffs and, far below, the sandy bed of the canyon.

"They won't find us here," Hermann remarked.

It was a relief to realize this, but also slightly frightening. This was a total wilderness, where even the hardiest animals struggled to survive. How could they be sure they would manage it?

It was too late to turn back. Leaving the truck at the top of the cliffs, the men followed a zebra track into the canyon, looking for water and a place to live. The riverbed was dry – there had been no rain that year. But there were still enough waterholes. To their delight, one of them contained fish – fat, healthy carp. They drove one into the corner of the muddy pool, where Hermann managed to grab it with his bare hands. Their first catch! They immediately lit a fire, and cooked and ate it.

They continued through the canyon until they came to a kind of cave, an overhanging rock that provided ample shelter. They decided that this would be their home. Over the next two days, they moved supplies from their truck, and made the cave as comfortable as they could. Then they hid the truck under an overhanging cliff so that it wouldn't be visible from the air.

They were feeling desperately hungry. They had eaten some of their pasta supplies, but they dared not eat more. They allowed themselves a cup of flour each day for breakfast, mixed with water, along with a spoonful of jam. There was nothing else to do: they had to find more food.

The obvious solution was to catch more fish, but this was easier said than done. The luck of their first day wasn't repeated. They made fishing hooks with wire, but all they caught were frogs. With their stomachs rumbling, they decided to go hunting. The fight for survival had begun.

On their way into the canyon, they had spotted the tracks of some wild cattle − a bull, a cow and a calf. To their delight, they soon stumbled upon the bull, grazing on the floor of the canyon. But how could they get close enough to shoot?

"I'll go back this way with Otto and the shotgun," said Henno. "You go ahead with the pistol. My scent will drive him in your direction."

It was a good idea. Henno set off carefully, not wanting to disturb the massive creature. He crept closer, and closer… and then the bull looked up. He saw Henno, and charged. Henno fired the shotgun straight at the bull's face. It still kept coming. At the last minute, Henno leapt up onto a rocky ledge, out of its way. The bull glared at him. The small shotgun pellets (generally used only for small game such as birds) had barely scratched him.

But now Hermann ran up and fired his pistol. The bullet hit the bull behind the ear, and the huge animal dropped to the ground like a stone.

Two men and a dog

"Is he dead?" gasped Hermann.

Henno threw a stone at its head, just to be sure. Immediately, the bull got back to his feet – very much alive! Now Otto, wildly excited, threw himself at the bull and grasped his nose. Hermann stepped closer, and shot the bull in the forehead. It had no effect. The bull simply tossed his head, throwing Otto into the air as he did so.

Otto got to his feet again, but now he was whimpering. Hunting wasn't as much fun as he'd expected. Hermann shot the bull once more behind the ear. As before, this stunned him and he dropped to the ground again – only to get up when he'd recovered.

He was definitely weaker now, only able to glare at the men balefully. They felt slightly sick. They were out of pistol bullets, because they had not expected this to be such a gruesome, long-winded battle.

"We'll have to go and get more bullets," said Hermann. "And work out how to finish him off."

Henno nodded. "We should bring our sleeping bags, too, and anything else we'll need. He's too big to carry up to the cave. We'll have to stay here until we've eaten him."

So they scrambled back to their home, bringing back knives, ropes, a frying pan and other essentials. The bull was now lying down, but scrambled to his feet and charged again as they approached. Two more bullets still didn't kill him. They knew they should aim for his heart. "*But where exactly was the heart in that enormous body?"* wrote Henno later. *"Neither Hermann nor I had ever slaughtered an ox and we had no idea… By this time Hermann and I were both quite shaken. It was a shocking business and our inability to end it made us feel ashamed."*

Eventually, they had the idea of slinging a rope around the bull's horns and tying the rope to a tree, so that he couldn't move. Then, with great relief, they slit his throat.

They gorged themselves on meat that night. But now came the task of preserving the rest of the carcass. It would quickly go bad in the hot sun. So they carved it up, discovering as they did so that none of their bullets had actually gone through the creature's tough skull. They cut part of the flesh into thin strips to dry, making *biltong*, as it is called throughout southern Africa. The rest had to be smoked over a slow-burning fire. It was a tricky technique to master; the men had to make several attempts before they got it right. And then it was wild bull for breakfast, lunch and dinner for many, many days to come.

Killing the bull was their first major encounter with the difficulties of hunting. They quickly learned that it was a cruel, desperate way to live. With their own limited resources, they had to think first of their own needs, and could not afford any kindness. Frequently, their bullets only wounded an animal, and they would have to trail it for hours to finish it off. Often it got away altogether. When it was injured badly enough, they would simply have to wait for it to weaken and lie down. They could not waste their precious bullets on giving it a quick, clean death.

The constant diet of meat rapidly became tiresome, and they worked on new ways of catching the carp in the waterhole. Eventually they hit upon the ingenious idea of making a net with tamarisk branches and pairs of underpants, which they then trawled through the water between them. It worked – and for a while, they had plenty of fish suppers.

But the waterhole was gradually drying up. This source of food would clearly not last forever. What was more, they realized that someone was sharing it with them. The carp were being attacked in the night. Footprints revealed the culprit – a hyena.

A hyena

Henno was furious. "I'm not letting him get away with this!" he announced. "I'm going to lie in wait for him and shoot him."

"Don't be silly," said Hermann. "If you're anywhere near, he'll smell you. And anyway, you won't be able to shoot him in the dark."

But Henno was determined. He took his sleeping bag to the waterhole and settled down to wait.

On the first night, nothing happened. Henno returned to the cave empty-handed in the morning, and Hermann greeted him with an amused smile and a cup of coffee. He clearly didn't think that his friend would try again. But Henno, annoyed at his attitude, took up guard again the next night.

He was just dozing off when he heard the bloodcurdling howl of the hyena, close at hand. He reached for the shotgun as the hyena continued to screech and cackle. It was terrible; no other animal in the desert makes a sound anything like it. But it was just what Henno needed. Even though he couldn't see the beast, he simply aimed in the general direction of the noise. To his glee, the howling stopped and an injured yelping took its place.

"Got it!" he thought and, curling over in his sleeping bag, he slept soundly until morning.

By daylight, he got up and surveyed the scene. There was strange-looking trail, which suggested that the hyena could no longer use its hind legs. Henno wondered how far it could get by dragging itself along. He followed the trail until he eventually found the brute cowering under an acacia tree.

He didn't want to waste another bullet. Instead, he began to pound the back of its head with stones. It was another long, gruesome battle before the hyena finally collapsed. Exhausted, but feeling he had somehow triumphed, Henno skinned the animal and took its pelt back to the cave. Hermann didn't laugh at him this time.

The days passed, blending into one another. Henno and Hermann watched the changing seasons, and had to make their own adjustments. Their carp pond dried up, and they began to get headaches from the lack of vitamins in their diet. They realized that, to correct this, they would need to drink more blood and eat raw meat. Ever inventive, they made sausages from the blood of a gemsbok, using its intestines as the skin.

A gemsbok

They also begin to run out of salt, and water – two of the essentials for survival. Just like the animals around them, they had to move to find both. Nothing was going to come to them in their cave. So they marched through the parched canyons, staving off thirst and hunger, until they found salt deposits and fresh waterholes.

On one of these marches, they sheltered for a while under a rock face to cool off. The ground where they sat was infested with sand ticks, as many animals had used this shady spot before them.

"I think a tick just got me," said Hermann suddenly, shaking his hand. The tick had bitten him on the palm – not surprising, in the circumstances. But within a few seconds, he began to keel over.

"Hermann!" said Henno, alarmed, as Hermann slumped to the ground. "Are you all right?"

"My head…" groaned Hermann. Henno stared at him. He had come out in a strange rash, all over his body. Quickly, Henno hunted for the tick that had bitten him.

"Look at this!" he exclaimed, when he found it. The tick was full of old, black blood. Hermann clearly had acute blood poisoning from its bite – and wasn't capable of looking at anything. He vomited violently.

"I can't see," he muttered. "My eyesight's going."

Panicking, Henno slashed open the tick bite and crammed some permanganate of potash (a kind of antiseptic) into the wound. There was nothing else he could do. Hermann could barely stand, and was now half-blind, but Henno got him into a small cave nearby. They spent the rest of the day and the night there, waiting for the poisoning to subside.

It was not until the next afternoon that Hermann felt well enough to move again. It was a frightening incident, showing them just how fragile their lives were in the wilderness.

As the seasons wore on, their fortunes changed. There were droughts, and they were forced to abandon their first home in search of water; they lived in several places, setting up camp wherever there was enough water to keep them alive. There were also times of plenty after the occasional rains, which brought the desert dramatically to life. Henno later described the tremendous power of a flash flood, and the beautiful sight of four thousand springbok grazing together after the rains.

A springbok

Throughout it all, Otto stayed with them. He never tired of hunting, even though he was twice impaled on a gemsbok's horns. He learned survival methods just as the men did, and they marvelled at how all animals, even domesticated ones, adapt to their changing surroundings.

But overall, they were getting weaker, and they were constantly hungry. As a second dry season took its toll, they found that they were almost too weak to hunt.

They grew desperate. One day, a big lizard scuttled past, and Henno lunged at it. He caught it by the tail just as it got halfway into some rocks. "*That lizard provided us with two good meals,*" he wrote. "*The flesh was firm and white and tasted like a cross between chicken and salmon.*"

And then Hermann began to get seriously ill. He suffered from pains in his back, which gradually spread to his legs, and eventually to his neck and head. Henno did his best to take care of him, shooting fresh game, which they ate raw. But nothing seemed to help.

Hermann obviously needed to see a doctor. He could no longer hunt, and could barely even crawl around. There was only one thing to do. They would have to leave the desert, after all they had been through. With a heavy heart, Henno prepared the truck and drove the treacherous way back to Windhoek.

Afterwards

Henno didn't give himself up immediately. He dropped Hermann off and went back into the desert with Otto. But friends persuaded Hermann to tell them where he was hiding, and the police soon found him.

As they had expected, the two men were interned in prison; but not for long. They were transferred to a hospital, where Hermann began to recover. He had been suffering from a deficiency of Vitamin B.

Then they had to stand trial. There were many charges against them, large and small, including failure to pay their dog licence. But they were lucky. Their adventure had been so extraordinary that they got off with a few small fines.

Tragically, after making a full recovery, Hermann Korn was killed in a car accident in 1946. Otto lived on for a few years, then mysteriously disappeared. Henno Martin continued to live in Namibia, and wrote a book about their two and a half years in the Namib. It is called *The Sheltering Desert*, and this story is based upon his account.

The real
Indiana Jones

As the long line of camels set off in the shadow of the Great Wall of China, the men leading them began a strange, eerie chant, a prayer for safety from evil spirits. The heavily laden camels were bound for the vast expanses of the Gobi Desert in Mongolia, and in spite of their chant, the men all carried rifles. They knew they would have more than spirits to worry about before their journey was over.

A tall, athletic man watched the 75 camels pace away from him. When he was sure that they were safely on their way, he turned and walked briskly across to his car. He had a lot to do. The camels were only part of a vast expedition that he had organized. His name was Roy Chapman Andrews, and he was one of America's most famous 20th-century explorers.

Roy Chapman Andrews was 38 years old, and he had already established a reputation as a fearless, daring adventurer. He had explored many parts of the Far East and South-East Asia, and had spent two weeks stranded on a desert island. He had killed a 20-foot python, hunted man-eating tigers, and seen the opium dens of Japan; he had narrowly escaped death by poisoned bamboo stake, by typhoon at sea and by shark attack. To add to his fame, he had been an American spy in the Far East during the First World War, and was not merely an adventurer, but a zoologist, with a skill for stuffing animals and a unique understanding of whales. Now, in March 1922, he was about to begin the biggest adventure of his entire career.

Andrews was based at the American Museum of Natural History in New York. Its director, Henry Osborn, believed that the earliest humans had come not from Africa, but from the heart of Asia. But there was no proof of this. So Andrews made a daring proposal. Why not send a major expedition to the Gobi Desert, to test the truth of Osborn's theory? It could take place over five summers, with Andrews at the head of a varied, experienced team of scientists. Osborn was delighted with the idea – and Andrews was the ideal man to carry it out.

When the American press found out, there was a frenzy of excitement. "*Scientists to seek Ape-man's bones,*" announced *The New York Times*. " *'Missing Link': Expedition to seek remains of near-man in Gobi wilds,*" claimed *The Washington Post*. Donations from the wealthiest people in New York began to flood in, quickly amassing the $250,000 needed – an enormous sum at the time, more than $5 million in today's money. And about ten thousand people wrote to Andrews, begging to join the expeditions.

Even so, as he watched his camel train begin its slow, dignified procession out into the desert, it seemed incredible to Andrews that his idea was becoming a reality... The Central Asiatic Expeditions, as they came to be known, were actually happening.

The camels carried the supplies for Andrews and the other scientists, who followed in five Dodge cars several weeks later. They set off on April 17, 1922, from their base in Kalgan, China, into what Andrews liked to call the 'Great Unknown'. He was well aware that they were taking an enormous risk – the fact was that hardly any fossils had ever been found in Mongolia. But the pressure was on for Andrews to discover some now.

The Gobi Desert was full of dangers, especially then. Wild, inhospitable and immensely varied, it was full of pitfalls for the Dodge vehicles, which often sank up to their axles in soft ground or sand. There were vast gravel plains, craggy buttes and rocky outcrops, and areas of sweeping sand dunes. The climate was also wildly changeable; temperatures could drop to well below freezing, and storms of all kinds were a constant threat. Sandstorms in particular could arise unexpectedly, howling viciously and wrecking everything in their path.

The Dodge vehicles depended heavily on the camel train, which carried fuel, oil and spare parts; but even for the camels, surviving in the desert wasn't easy. There was often little that they could eat, and with no food they quickly weakened under their heavy loads.

But, above all, both camels and Dodge vehicles had to deal with the threat of bandits. The political situation in both China and Mongolia was unstable. With unrest and civil war breaking out constantly, there were increasing numbers of marauding bandits, who sometimes joined together in wild, ruthless gangs of up to a thousand men. They raided anything of value that passed through the Gobi, killing without mercy. Andrews' men had to be constantly on their guard; they all carried shotguns and pistols.

But as this first season got underway, the scientists soon forgot the dangers. There were so many species of animals in the desert to record. The team watched wild asses, which roamed freely in great herds. Scientists had known of their existence, but had never before had the opportunity to observe them close up. Andrews shot several as exhibits, and took detailed notes of how they behaved. More importantly, though, the scientists began to find fossils. Fossils of ancient creatures: fish, toads, insects, rodents and other small mammals, long extinct.

But what about early man? Nothing. No human-like fossils were found at all. Instead, there was something else – something unexpected. *Dinosaurs*. And not just any old dinosaurs. These were new species, never seen before. One of the first to emerge from the eroded rock formations was a strange creature from the Cretaceous period (between 135 and 65 million years ago), with a beak like a parrot. They named it *Psittacosaurus mongoliensis*, which means 'parrot lizard from Mongolia'.

The team was very excited. They didn't have to worry any longer about returning from the desert empty-handed. They worked feverishly, desperate to make the most of their finds. But, towards September, the temperatures began to drop and the Gobi became ever more threatening. They would have to leave, and return in the spring. The first season was at an end – or so they thought...

While hunting for the northbound road to Mongolia's capital, Urga, the team got lost in a vast area of desert. It seemed never-ending. For three days they hunted for some signs of life, or clues as to where to go. Eventually, they spotted a small group of Mongol nomads' huts, known as *yurts*. Andrews drove over to see if they could help, leaving the others to await news. While he waited, the photographer, Shackelford, got out of his Dodge to stretch his legs. There was a strange outcropping of rock nearby, and he wandered over for a closer look.

What he found was astonishing. Before him lay a huge basin of dramatic sandstone cliffs, carved into fantastic shapes by years of erosion. "*There appear to be medieval castles with spires and turrets, brick-red in the evening light, colossal gateways, walls and ramparts...*" wrote Andrews.

The real Indiana Jones

It was stunning. But more importantly, lying casually on the surface of the rocks, lay fossils. Hundreds of them. Very excited, the team pitched their tents immediately, and began to explore. It was, as Andrews put it, 'a paradise for palaeontologists'. They named the spot the 'Flaming Cliffs'.

Hurriedly, the scientists gathered what they could. Among their finds was a piece of fossilized eggshell – perhaps left by some ancient bird? But it was a race against time. Soon, they would have to tear themselves away and, with the guidance of the local people, continue on to the capital. Freezing winds and even blasts of snow were beginning to assault the Gobi. They had to get out before the desert engulfed them.

But now they knew that the Flaming Cliffs awaited them on their return.

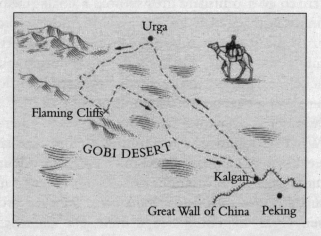

This map shows the expedition's route to the Flaming Cliffs.

The American Museum and the New York press were waiting for news of the expedition with great excitement. Andrews was never shy, and loved publicizing his exploits. As soon as he reached Urga he sent a long cable. "*Scientific results surpassed our greatest hopes,*" he announced.

Osborn was completely delighted at the news. He wrote back, "*You have written a new chapter in the history of life upon the earth.*" Andrews had done it again. His reputation soared. By the time the winter was over and it was time to begin the second expedition, he had become a household name in America.

In April 1923, Andrews and his team were back in Kalgan, China. They soon discovered that the dangers had not diminished since their last trip. If anything, the threat of bandits had grown worse. Some Russian traders had recently been robbed and brutally murdered, and the Kalgan soldiers did a poor job of keeping things under control. The scientists knew they had to keep their eyes open, and keep plenty of guns on show, to ward off the bandits.

They didn't have to wait long for the danger to surface. As Andrews was driving along near the spot where the Russians had been ambushed, he suddenly spotted the glint of sunlight on a gun barrel. It came from the top of a hill nearby. A bandit! As he drove closer, Andrews could see a man on horseback. Hurriedly, he drew his pistol and fired. The horseman disappeared. But as the car rounded a corner, Andrews saw that there was now not one horseman, but three.

Andrews thought quickly. There wasn't time to turn the car around, and if he did he would be fired upon anyway. "*Knowing that a Mongol pony would never stand against the charge of a motor car, I instantly decided to attack,*" he wrote later.

He was right. He drove at full speed at the horses, the car engine roaring. The bandits' horses panicked, and began to buck and rear in terror. The bandits, unable to reach their guns, began to panic, too. There was only one thing they could do – they turned and galloped away as fast as they could.

The team had survived. For now, there were no more bandit attacks – just the long, gruelling trek through the desert to the Flaming Cliffs, where the scientists were eager to continue searching for fossils. As soon as they had set up camp, the hunt began.

The previous season had given the team great hopes, and they were not disappointed. The fossilized bones lying around were quickly discovered to be whole skeletons and well-preserved skulls. Many of them were of a strange Cretaceous creature that had walked on all fours, and had a bizarre bony head, ending in a curved, parrot-like beak. The scientists named it *Protoceratops andrewsi*, after their intrepid leader. Roughly, it means 'Andrews' first horned-face dinosaur'.

But a more revolutionary discovery was yet to come. On July 13, 1923, one of the scientists, George Olsen, made an announcement as everyone sat down for lunch.

"I found some fossilized eggs this morning," he said casually.

Everyone stared at him. It didn't seem possible – they had now established that the fossil bed was from the Cretaceous period, which was too early for large birds. And as far as anyone knew at the time, dinosaurs didn't lay eggs. "*We did not take his story very seriously,*" wrote Andrews. But after lunch, they all went to see what he had found. The chief palaeontologist, Walter Granger, couldn't believe his eyes. There was no doubt that the fossils lying before them were eggs – but not birds' eggs.

"They're reptiles' eggs!" he exclaimed. "And that means… they have to be dinosaur eggs."

The discovery was groundbreaking. "*It was evident that dinosaurs did lay eggs and that we had discovered the first specimens known to science,*" wrote Andrews. It was wildly exciting.

And there was more. As the nest of eggs was uncovered, another skeleton was found – not of a Protoceratops, but of an odd, birdlike creature. It seemed to have died in the very act of raiding the nest of eggs. The men named it *Oviraptor philoceratops*, which means 'egg thief that loves horned-face dinosaurs'. The Central Asiatic Expeditions were truly surpassing all expectations.

But amid all the excitement, Andrews was feeling worried. While the Dodge cars had arrived at the Flaming Cliffs safely, the supply camels were late. The camp was running out of food. This didn't make life too difficult at the time, as there were plenty of antelopes to shoot – but things would get serious if the team was stranded in the desert over winter. And, in any case, what had happened to the caravan? Had the camels died on the way? Or had the whole caravan been attacked by bandits?

Andrews sent out some of his Mongol helpers to search for the camels. But this almost ended in disaster. One of them was attacked, and nearly killed. He made it back to the Flaming Cliffs barely alive. Things were not looking good. By now, Andrews was even prepared to listen to the words of an old wise man who was passing, and who claimed to be an expert astrologist.

"The caravan is still far away," the old man said. "The camels are dying. But you will receive news within three days."

Strangely, the old man was not far wrong. Four days later, one of the searchers found the caravan. The camel drivers had been unable to find food for the camels in the parched desert. They had gone out of their way to find grazing, but even so, many of the camels had died. When the caravan finally arrived at the Flaming Cliffs, only 39 of the 75 camels were still alive. It was a grim reminder of the dangers they all faced.

However, with enough fuel in camp, the team members now knew they could get back to civilization. The vast numbers of fossils were carefully loaded onto the backs of the remaining camels. The news of dinosaur eggs was about to hit the world.

Back in America, Andrews received a hero's welcome. Everyone had dinosaur fever. And Andrews' ambition was growing. The Central Asiatic Expeditions should continue for ten years, not five! He began a whirlwind fundraising tour that included 'auctioning' one of the egg fossils. It fetched $5,000, an enormous sum at the time.

But all the publicity had a negative effect, too. The Mongolian officials suddenly became aware that Andrews was taking many things of value from the Gobi Desert, and that they were getting little in return. Getting permission for his expeditions would gradually prove more and more difficult.

Nevertheless, in early 1925 Andrews was back. He battled with the Mongolian officials for permission, and eventually they gave in. But, from now on, he was under increasing pressure to leave his discoveries in Mongolia, and not to ship them to America. Andrews was fiercely patriotic and the Mongolians' attitude infuriated him.

Mongolian officials were not his only problem that season. Sandstorms raged, and the camel caravan lost many camels. Moving on from the Flaming Cliffs, the terrain of sand dunes, canyons and rocks was often impossible to cross with the trucks.

And then, near the end of the season, when the nights were getting colder, the camp had some very unwelcome visitors. Andrews was the first to spot the danger. Snakes! There were three venomous pit vipers slithering towards the tents, attracted by the warmth inside. He raised the alarm – none too soon. There were vipers everywhere: around people's bedposts, in their shoes…

The men attacked the snakes viciously, using tools, guns, hatchets or whatever came to hand. Incredibly, no one was bitten. In total, they killed 47 vipers between them. But the problem didn't go away. The scientists were forced to break camp, and move on. The desert winter was once more forcing them back to civilization.

Yet despite the problems, Andrews was proving that the Gobi Desert was indeed, as he himself had put it, "a paradise for palaeontologists". But now that he was not the only one to realize this, his dream of ten years of excavations began to fade. Neither the Chinese nor the Mongolians were happy about his activities. Moreover, the political situation in both China and Mongolia remained explosive. Civil war broke out in China, and Andrews witnessed many terrible atrocities in Peking and elsewhere. He himself narrowly avoided being shot by some ruthless Chinese soldiers. The 1926 season had to be abandoned.

Determined not to give in, Andrews managed to get another expedition going in 1927. Everything seemed to conspire against it: the Chinese civil war, the authorities (such as they were), increasing numbers of bandits, and wild, wild weather in the Gobi Desert that smashed equipment and ripped up tents. Work on finding fossils in these conditions was almost impossible.

And then Andrews accidentally shot himself. He was hunting antelopes, and had his revolver slung over his hip. Somehow, he pressed the trigger and the revolver exploded into his left leg. The bullet ripped through his thigh and came out underneath his knee. Fortunately, the team doctor did an excellent job of treating the wound, but Andrews had to recover under terrible conditions. The sandstorms raged constantly, causing everyone intense discomfort. "*Often I had to bury my head in the blankets to keep from screaming,*" he wrote.

Faced with such immense difficulties, there were no more trips for three years. Then, in 1930, Andrews led one more Central Asiatic Expedition into the desert. Again, in spite of all the dangers, there were incredible discoveries. One was of a creature like a huge elephant, with enormous, flat, shovel-like teeth at the end of its trunk. The scientists named it *Platybelodon* (which means 'shovel-tusked elephant') and were delighted to find a mother and baby, lying close together.

But it was becoming clear that the Expeditions' days were at an end. The resistance from the Chinese authorities grew too great. Andrews was forced to leave China for the last time in 1932. He returned to America, where his glowing reputation ensured a glittering career as a public speaker, writer and, eventually, director of the American Museum of Natural History.

Afterwards

The expeditions never did find the 'Missing Link'. Osborn's theory was false – or still remains to be proved. But the discoveries of dinosaurs were some of the greatest ever made.

Later discoveries showed that the dinosaur eggs were not those of Protoceratops, as Andrews and his team had thought. They belonged to *Oviraptor philoceratops*, the dinosaur they had found 'raiding' the nest. So Oviraptor was not in the act of thieving the eggs, but sitting on them.

It was also not quite true that these were the first dinosaur eggs ever found. In 1859, a clutch of eggs had been discovered in the French Pyrenees. A paper had been written about them, but it had been largely ignored at the time.

Thanks to movies like *Jurassic Park*, most people now know about some of the dinosaurs discovered by Andrews. The best known is the *Velociraptor* (which means 'quick thief'), the vicious carnivore that is featured in the movie, with its razor-sharp teeth and lethal hunter's instinct.

And what about Indiana Jones? Many have compared Roy Chapman Andrews to this fictional action film hero, and suggested that he was the original model. The creator of *Indiana Jones*, George Lucas, has always denied it. But there is no doubt that Andrews captured the imagination of a whole generation of Americans as the fearless, intrepid explorer who would let nothing stand in his way. There was no one quite like him, before or after; so it is easy to see how he might have influenced a writer, perhaps unconsciously.

Roy Chapman Andrews died on March 11, 1960, at the age of 76.

A desert disguise

"*I am only an eccentric, a dreamer anxious to live a free and nomadic life, far away from the civilized world...*" wrote Isabelle Eberhardt in June 1901, making her life sound very simple and romantic. It was far from being either. She led a strange, difficult existence, seeking answers to life's questions in the harsh sun of the Sahara Desert. She broke all the rules that women of her time were supposed to follow; she deeply shocked some people and inspired thousands of others. After her death, she became known as 'the Amazon of the Sahara' or, to some, 'the good nomad'.

Isabelle was born in Switzerland in February 1877. Her mother was a Russian exile, who had left her husband, a Russian general, in 1871. She never admitted who Isabelle's father was. She gave her new daughter her maiden name – Eberhardt.

Her father was probably the family tutor, Alexander Trophimowsky, a strange, intense man who had a big influence on Isabelle's childhood. They lived in a rambling villa outside Geneva, where there were few home comforts. Trophimowsky refused to send Isabelle or her sister and three brothers to school, or allow them beyond the grounds of the villa, so they were isolated from the outside world. They all spoke French and Russian, and Trophimowsky also taught Isabelle German, Latin, Italian and a little English, as well as Arabic.

In this strange environment, Isabelle became a dreamer, wandering around the grounds of the villa on her own. She read many, many books, and became interested in the Muslim religion, Islam, when she was quite young. She lived in a fantasy world, and got used to inventing new identities for herself. Trophimowsky encouraged her to dress as a boy, with her hair cropped short. Who was she? Who was her father? She was never really sure…

Through it all, she developed a longing to escape; and the place she longed to see was North Africa, and the Sahara Desert. Eventually she persuaded her mother to make a trip with her. They set off in May 1897 for Bône (now Annaba), in northern Algeria.

It was here that Isabelle began to create her 'desert' identity. She dressed as a young man, calling herself Si Mahmoud Saadi, and claimed to be a Tunisian scholar of the Koran (the holy book of Islam). In this disguise, she could mingle freely with the people of Bône, and quickly picked up the Algerian Arabic that was spoken on the streets. She felt perfectly safe, and very much at home.

But the dream couldn't last. Isabelle's mother died in Bône, and Isabelle was forced to return to Geneva. Within a year, her old tutor Trophimowsky had died, too, leaving her a small amount of money. Isabelle could now do as she pleased. When her grief had subsided, she realized she was free to go back to her beloved North Africa.

She set off in June 1899 for Tunis. There, she became Si Mahmoud Saadi once again, and made plans to fulfil her lifelong dream – to go to the desert.

In Tunisia and Algeria at the end of the 19th century, there were no easy roads connecting the desert towns. The only way for Isabelle to reach her destination, Ouargla in Algeria, was on horseback, accompanied by guides on donkeys.

It was an eventful journey. There was little water to be found along the route, and Isabelle suffered constantly from thirst and a high fever. Even where there were wells, they were not always easy to find, especially if the party arrived at night. On one occasion, they hunted for a well in total darkness, with matches as the only light to guide them. She and her guides slept under the stars, wrapped in their *burnous*, the cloaks worn by people of the region.

It took them eight days to reach the town of Touggourt – a journey of 220km (135 miles). Isabelle was welcomed there, and she made inquiries about heading further south to Ouargla. But the further she went, the more dangerous her trip would become, and the French authorities were keeping a closer eye on her than she imagined. The nomadic people of the desert, the Tuareg, had already killed a number of Europeans who had naively believed they would be welcomed; so it was perhaps not surprising that the French authorities refused to give Isabelle permission to go further south.

Instead, she made the journey to the Souf, part of the Great Eastern Erg, which comprises a number of oases set amongst undulating white sand dunes and salt pans. The principal town in the Souf is El Oued, and this was Isabelle's destination. It was another difficult desert crossing – it took five days to complete the 100km (60-mile) journey.

But, once she was there, the oasis enchanted her. To this day, El Oued is one of the most beautiful towns in Algeria, known also as the 'City of a Thousand Domes' because of its architecture. Its domed houses are painted white, its palm groves are green and lush, and the Sahara is just at hand, its beautiful sands stretching out in every direction. For Isabelle, it felt like home.

Isabelle completed her round trip in a few weeks: an extraordinary journey for a European woman at that time. What was even more amazing was that she was openly welcomed by the local people she met – especially the religious leaders. Was it because of her disguise, perhaps? In a way… but Isabelle was different from many Europeans, in that she genuinely wanted to be part of North African life. She was not like the French invaders who had taken over the country; she believed in Islam passionately, and could talk intelligently about the Koran and Islamic beliefs.

A desert disguise

This map shows the parts of the desert Isabelle visited.

The religious leaders probably knew that they were talking to a woman, but they forgave her because she clearly believed everything she said.

She headed back to Europe, but it was not long before the desert drew her back again. This time, she decided that she would not just make a trip. She would return to the desert to live.

El Oued had captured her heart. There, she thought, she could lead a life of tranquillity; she could concentrate on being a writer and developing her Muslim faith. She would be surrounded by the sights and sounds that she loved.

"*Oh Sahara, menacing Sahara, hiding your dark and beautiful soul in bleak, desolate emptiness!*" she wrote. "*Oh yes, I love this country of sand and stone, this country*

*of camels and primitive men and vast, treacherous salt-
flats."*

So, after another long, tiring journey, she arrived in
El Oued and rented a house. She exulted in her
arrival. *"I am far away from all people, far from civilization
and its hypocritical shams. I am alone, on the soil of Islam,
out in the desert, free..."* she wrote happily.

She settled into a simple life, mingling with the
people and meeting the local holy men. She bought
a horse and named him Souf, after the region, and
wandered the white sand dunes at night on
horseback. She wrote of the beauty of the dunes and
of the sunsets over the desert: *"To the west... the sun
was a veritable ball of blood sinking in a blaze of gold and
crimson. The slopes of the dunes seemed to be on fire below
the ridges, in hues that deepened from one moment to the
next."*
She was often accompanied into the dunes by an
Algerian soldier named Slimène, who later became
her husband – although this friendship was one of
the many reasons why some people thought badly of
her. On the whole, Europeans thought of themselves
as superior to North Africans, and kept themselves
apart from them. Most found the idea of a European
actually marrying an Algerian totally shocking. But
with Slimène, and living in El Oued, Isabelle was
happier than she had ever been in her life.
At this time, she took her Muslim faith a step
further. She got to know the leaders of the oldest Sufi

sect in the world – the Qadrya brotherhood. Sufism is a mystical form of Islam, and only selected people can become members of its sects. The two leaders of the Qadrya, Sidi el Hussein and Sidi el Hachemi, warmed to Isabelle, although it's almost certain that they saw through her disguise. Before long, they initiated her into the sect – something completely unheard of for a European, let alone a woman.

But Isabelle's dream of a tranquil life was not to last. She was, in fact, rather naïve to think that she could just disappear into the desert. The French authorities knew about her even before she arrived and, without her knowing it, she was kept under careful surveillance all the time that she lived in El Oued. Why were they so suspicious of her? She was doing no one any harm.

The problem was that the French rulers in Algeria were afraid of the people around them. They feared that the Algerians might rise against them, and fight for their freedom. Isabelle, although a European, was a Muslim and loved the local people. Some thought that she might encourage them to rebel against the French. And in any case, the way she lived was shocking – dressing as a man, wandering around on her own… and despite what she thought, Isabelle's relationship with Slimène was no secret, either. There were mutterings that Isabelle represented a threat on many levels, not only to the authorities, but to people's ideas of decency, too.

In the meantime, Isabelle's 'idyllic' life was growing harsher. The weather in the Sahara could be ferocious – winds whipped up the sand, blasting the houses and making life very uncomfortable. In winter, it was also surprisingly cold. And Isabelle had run out of money. She had always intended to establish herself as a writer and earn money that way, but it wasn't easy. Now, she was in debt. She was often ill, and rarely ate enough.

Then came some bad news. The army was sending Slimène away from El Oued, to the town of Batna, further north. Isabelle didn't know it, but the authorities hoped that, by sending him away, they could get rid of her. They were sure that she would follow Slimène – and they were right.

But before she left, a terrible and extraordinary event took place. She went to visit some of her Sufi friends, and stopped off in a village called Béhima. There, she was welcomed into the house of a local wealthy man, and sat in his courtyard surrounded by members of the Qadrya. As she sat quietly among them, helping a young man translate a letter, she suddenly felt a violent blow to her head.

Before she had time to think or react, there were two more blows, this time to her left arm. She looked up and saw a man wildly waving a weapon over her head, as her Qadrya friends leaped to defend her. Shocked and dazed, Isabelle herself jumped up and ran to the wall, where a sword was hanging. Her friends had already wrestled the man's weapon from him, but he himself escaped, and ran off.

"I shall bring back a gun to finish her off!" he was heard to cry as he disappeared.

The Qadryas returned to Isabelle, who was bleeding heavily from her wounds.

"This is what the cur wounded you with!" cried one of them, showing her a sword that was dripping with blood.

There was no doubt who the attacker was. Several of the people present had recognized him, although Isabelle herself did not. His name was Abdallah Mohammed ben Lakhdar, and he came from the village of Béhima itself. He belonged to another Sufi sect called the Tidjanya brotherhood, the greatest rival sect to the Qadryas. The leader of the Tidjanyas was quickly summoned, and was told to hunt the man out. At first he refused.

"If you don't find him, we will say you are an accomplice to the crime," he was told. Reluctantly, he sent people to find Abdallah – not a difficult task in a village so small. Abdallah was caught, and brought to the wealthy man's house where Isabelle still lay injured.

A bizarre scene followed. Abdallah was brought into the room where Isabelle lay bleeding on a mattress. She had still received no treatment for her wounds, which were quite serious. Instead, Abdallah was interrogated in front of her, and she joined in herself with more questions.

"Why have you done such a terrible thing?" he was asked.

At first, Abdallah pretended to be mad. But none of the local people believed him, because they knew him well. So he dropped the sham, and simply stated that God had sent him to kill Isabelle.

"But you don't know me," said Isabelle. "And I don't know you."

"No," agreed Abdallah. "I have never seen you before. But I must kill you, nevertheless. If these people set me free, I would try to do so again."

"Why?" asked Isabelle. "What do you have against me?"

"Nothing. You have done me no wrong. I don't know you, but I must kill you."

His responses made no sense at all.

"Do you know she is a Muslim?" asked one of the other men.

"Yes," said Abdallah.

It was all very mysterious. Several hours later, a doctor arrived from El Oued, and Isabelle was treated. She had been very lucky – a laundry line had deflected the blow to her head, which might easily have killed her otherwise. The worst injury was to her left elbow, which had been slashed through to the bone.

The delay in treating her meant that Isabelle had lost a lot of blood. She was very weak. The next day she was transferred to the military hospital in El

Oued, where she spent almost a month recovering. It was the end of her desert idyll. When she was well enough, she made her way north, to join Slimène in Batna.

In spite of what had happened, the French authorities were still determined to get rid of her. She was banished from Algeria, and only allowed to return for the trial of Abdallah, which took place four months later.

The trial did little to clear up the mystery. By this time, Abdallah seemed sorry for the attack, and begged Isabelle's forgiveness. But he still didn't explain why he had done it. Isabelle herself believed that he had been a paid assassin, employed either by the French authorities or by the Tidjanya Sufis. There was talk that he had been able to pay off his debts and buy a palm grove. But even if the gossip was true, he ended up paying a much higher price himself. The court convicted him of attempted murder, and he was sentenced to a lifetime of hard manual work.

Isabelle was appalled. It was a terrible sentence, especially as he had a wife and children. Believing that he was not the true criminal, she pleaded with the authorities to be more lenient. They responded by reducing Abdallah's sentence to ten years in jail.

After the trial, Isabelle was once more banished to France, where she lived with her brother in Marseilles. Slimène joined her there, and they were married. The marriage gave Isabelle the right to return to Algeria – but little did she know that it would be for the last time...

Isabelle found it difficult to stay in one place for long. Even in Algeria, the northern coastal towns didn't fully satisfy her yearnings. The desert, further south, always called her. When the opportunity arose to work with the French army south of the Atlas mountains, she jumped at the chance.

Isabelle's job was to travel around listening to the nomads and helping to smooth relations between them and the French colonials. It was strange work for her to take on, because she was not really a supporter of French rule. *"Whatever their unenlightened way of life, the lowliest of Bedouins are far superior to those idiotic Europeans making a nuisance of themselves,"* she wrote. But the section of the army she was working with wanted to proceed by persuasion and mutual understanding rather than force; perhaps she felt it was the better of two evils.

And, of course, the work allowed her to return to the desert. She moved from town to town, and lived for a while in a monastery, as she had the right to do as a Qadrya initiate.

But her health was suffering. As always when in the desert, she suffered from fevers, mostly caused by malaria, and they were getting worse. She was admitted to the military hospital in the town of Aïn Sefra, just where the Atlas mountains meet the Sahara Desert. She spent almost three weeks there in

A desert disguise

October 1904, before discharging herself.

Her husband Slimène, whose work had kept him in northern Algeria, came to be with her when she left hospital on October 20. Their reunion was a short one, because on October 21 a flash flood hit the town of Aïn Sefra.

The desert is a place of extremes. Most of the time it is terribly dry, terribly hot in the daytime and sometimes terribly cold at night. But when rains occur anywhere nearby, especially if there are mountains, the results can be devastating.

There had been no rains in Aïn Sefra in recent weeks. The *wadi*, the riverbed that ran through the town, was completely dry. But somewhere in the Atlas mountains there must have been rain, for suddenly, on the morning of October 21, there was a great roar and a ferocious torrent surged down the mountain, engulfing everything in its path. The yellow, turbulent waters picked up debris, tree trunks and bushes, crashing into houses and sweeping people away.

There was little time to react, and the flash flood subsided almost as quickly as it had appeared. Only then could the real damage be assessed. More than 20 people had died – and among them was Isabelle, found buried under rubble inside her house. Considering how much she had packed into her life, it is astonishing that she was only 27 years old when she died.

Afterwards

After her death, a friend gathered together all Isabelle's writings for publication. She became a romanticized heroine in Parisian circles – much was written about her, including two plays, and people still ponder her controversial life to this day.

What made her stand out among the 'desert adventurers' of her time, however, was her genuine desire to belong to the local people. She was not alone in adopting a disguise; the most famous example was the explorer Richard Burton, who disguised himself as a Muslim to enter the holy city of Mecca. But he was a Christian who merely wanted to enter a place that was otherwise forbidden to him. Isabelle was different. Although her identity as Si Mahmoud Saadi helped her to fit in, it was also an identity she felt comfortable with. She wasn't a man, and she wasn't Tunisian, but she *was* the Koranic scholar she claimed to be – and that was why the people of North Africa loved her.

Lawrence
of Arabia

The London audiences sat spellbound, hanging on every word.

"The wild sons of Ishmael regarded their quiet, fair-headed leader as a sort of supernatural being who had been sent from heaven to deliver them from their oppressors," the journalist told them. "He dressed in the garb of an Oriental ruler, and at his belt he carried the curved gold sword worn only by the direct descendants of the prophet Mohammed."

The people of London held their breaths. Who was this amazing, romantic British hero? Where was he now?

"The young man is at present flying from one part of London to another, trying to escape the fairer sex," the journalist assured them.

It was September 1919. The First World War was at an end, but at what a terrible cost. In Europe, millions of Britons, Frenchmen and Germans had died in a gruesome, drawn-out stalemate in muddy trenches. Britain and France had defeated Germany, but there seemed little to celebrate; the tales of trench warfare were just too horrible to think about.

But here was something different – a different

kind of war, with a different kind of hero: Lawrence of Arabia – who, if the journalist was to be believed, had led the Arabs single-handedly in a revolt against the Turks, riding majestically to victory across the desert, robes flying behind him as he charged ahead on his camel.

Far from running around London 'trying to escape the fairer sex', the real Lawrence – Thomas Edward Lawrence, to be precise – was sitting in Oxford, deeply depressed at what he saw as his failure to give the Arab people what they deserved. And, in the next few years, he tried his best to avoid the publicity caused by this well-meaning American journalist, whose name was Lowell Thomas.

First of all, he entered the Royal Air Force at a very low rank, under the assumed name of John Hume Ross. When the press found out his real identity, he changed his name again, this time to Thomas Edward Shaw, and joined the Tank Corps in the army. He returned to the Air Force under this name, still in the lower ranks, and spent the next 12 years in obscurity. His fellow servicemen never guessed who he was.

So what was the truth? Was 'Lawrence of Arabia' just a myth, created by a journalist who knew how badly the British needed a boost of morale? Or was there really something extraordinary about the quiet man who spent the rest of his life hiding from the press?

The truth lies somewhere in between. T. E. Lawrence began his career with an Oxford degree in history, and it was at this time that he developed an interest in the Middle East. He wrote a thesis on the Crusader castles of Palestine and Syria, journeying there for research, and began to learn Arabic. In 1910, after finishing his thesis, he returned to Syria to work on an archaeological dig at the ancient city of Carchemish. There, until the beginning of the First World War in 1914, he expanded his knowledge of the region and grew to love the people around him.

At that time, most of the Middle East was ruled by the Turks. Their empire (called the Ottoman empire) stretched from Turkey to modern-day Iraq. They were officially in control of Egypt, too. But the real power in Egypt was Britain, which kept a close eye on the Suez Canal – a vital route for its shipping.

This map shows the extent of the Ottoman empire at the time of the First World War.

When the First World War broke out, Turkey joined Austria and Germany against Russia, France and Britain. In the Arabian city of Mecca, the deposed *sherif* (Islamic leader), Sherif Hussein, now considered his options. He could back his Turkish rulers; or he could approach the British in the hope that they would help him gain independence for all the Arabic peoples, from the Arabian peninsula to Iraq and Syria.

The British liked the idea of having the Arabs on their side – it would help them in their battle against the Turks. They agreed with Hussein that if there was a successful Arab revolt, they would guarantee Arab independence after the war. So, on June 10, 1916, Hussein symbolically fired his rifle at the Turkish barracks in Mecca. The Arab Revolt had begun.

It was obvious that Sherif Hussein couldn't beat the Turks on his own. They had vast armies, and the sherif had only badly organized tribesmen. The British would have to launch a major offensive themselves, and give whatever help they could to the Arabs. So the British army sent representatives to Mecca, to see what was needed – and one of these was T. E. Lawrence.

At the start of the war, Lawrence had been posted to the British Intelligence department in Cairo, and he quickly became interested in the Arab Revolt. He decided that what the Revolt lacked was a leader. The sherif himself was a cantankerous old man, so

Lawrence visited the sherif's four sons to see what they were made of. Lawrence decided that the sherif's third son, the Emir Feisal, was the one with the necessary qualities. The two men got along well, and Lawrence was soon involved in helping him plan the desert campaign.

The Arab Revolt wouldn't stand a chance if it fought the conventional way, as a disciplined army. The Arab Bedouin were fierce warriors, but they belonged to many different tribes who tended to end up fighting each other. Wanting to understand them and learn about desert customs, Lawrence watched Feisal. He was impressed with Feisal's handling of tribal issues, which took a huge amount of patience. Gradually, he began to understand how to make the most of the Arabs' limited resources.

Before long, Lawrence had helped the Revolt to develop a strategy. They would use guerrilla warfare to attack the Hejaz railway, which ran through the desert, from Damascus in Syria right down to the holy city of Medina. There were vast stretches of desert track that the Turks could not possibly guard; and by disrupting their system of transport, the Arabs would hinder the Turkish war effort while losing very few men themselves. Other British officers agreed with the strategy, and supplied Lawrence with explosives and other artillery.

Very quickly, Lawrence became personally involved in the attacks against the railway. He understood how to use the explosives and, unlike many other British officers, seemed ideally suited to the desert war. He now spoke fluent Arabic, so he was able to communicate; he learned how to ride a camel and prided himself on enduring the harsh physical demands of life in the desert. It was Feisal who suggested to Lawrence that he wear Arab clothes. He gave him a beautiful set of robes made of pure white silk, which became part of the Lawrence 'image'; these helped him to mingle more effectively with the tribesmen.

On his trips, Lawrence was often accompanied by Arabs from different tribes, or even different countries. As a British officer in their midst, he had to act as mediator, resolving tribal issues along the way. On one of the early expeditions, a Moroccan killed a Bedouin tribesman. Knowing that this could spark a blood feud, in which tribal members were obliged to start killing in revenge, Lawrence realized that the only solution was for him to execute the Moroccan himself. Sick with fever and boils and weak from the hardships of the desert, he could hardly shoot straight, and took three shots to kill the man. It was a foretaste of things to come.

Meanwhile, Russia, France and Britain were secretly discussing what would happen if they won the war. Who would rule what, and where? France wanted to share out the former Ottoman empire with Britain. Despite the agreement with Sherif

Hussein, Britain felt obliged to agree. The result was the Sykes-Picot agreement of May 1916. According to this, France would rule Lebanon, Syria and part of Turkey, while Britain would rule Iraq and what is now Jordan. In other words, all the wealthy, highly populated areas would go to Britain and France, while the Arabs would get only the Arabian peninsula, which consisted mainly of desert.

One of the controversies surrounding Lawrence is whether he knew the terms of this agreement. He later denied that he did, but this denial was slightly unconvincing. He certainly had more than an inkling of its contents; in any case, it became public knowledge after the Russian Revolution of 1917, when the Russians published all their former agreements. His position seems to have rested on the hope that, once the war was over, the British would act justly to protect Arab interests. Lawrence was deeply loyal to Britain, and believed in British fair-mindedness. He didn't see why France should get a share of the Middle East when they hadn't done any of the fighting. If it was the Arabs themselves who defeated the Turks and entered Damascus, the British couldn't possibly allow the French to take their lands – could they?

So the Arab Revolt continued. Lawrence worked on plans for the Arab army to move north up the Arabian peninsula to Akaba, on the Red Sea – an important strategic port held by the Turks. It was well guarded from the sea, so the only hope of taking it was from inland, via the desert, and to use the weapon of surprise.

Lawrence found the help he needed in the form of a tribal leader named Auda abu Tayi, a hardened desert warrior. Lawrence suggested that they approach Akaba via an inland route. This way, they could recruit tribal support along the way, and they would never be spotted by the Turks. Auda agreed that it was feasible, and a small party set out from the town of Wedj on May 9, 1917.

The journey was tiring and difficult. There were long stretches of desert riding with little water. Lawrence himself fell ill again with boils and high fever, but struggled on. They crossed the Hejaz railway, blowing part of it up as they went. Then they spent a morning crossing the desolate mud flats of Biseita, a vast plain in the desert. Suddenly, they realized that one of the party was missing. His camel was still with the group – its rider had obviously dozed off in the searing heat and simply fallen off.

The missing man, Gasim, was part of Lawrence's own team. He realized with a sinking heart that he would have to go back and look for him personally, or lose the respect of the others. So he turned his camel, and forced it back across the mud flats.

Gasim was almost delirious from the desert heat when Lawrence found him. They caught up with the others, but were both near total exhaustion. What was worse, one of the tribal leaders beat Lawrence's servants for letting him go back alone. "*Think tonight was worst of my experience,*" wrote Lawrence in his diary.

After the hardships of trekking through the desert, Lawrence had the task of persuading other Arab tribes to join the Revolt. Fearing that the British might uphold the Sykes-Picot agreement, he felt terrible. "*We are calling them to fight for us on a lie, and I can't stand it,*" he wrote to one of his fellow-officers. But it was too late to change the plan. Fired by the idea of the Revolt, the Arab tribes were putting their weight behind it. By early July, they were close to Akaba.

The first encounter took place just north of Akaba, at Abu el Lissan. Taken by surprise, the Turks didn't know how to deal with the Arab snipers, who were hidden in the hills. When the Arabs eventually charged on their camels, the Turks simply panicked. A few days later, Akaba had fallen. It was now in Arab hands.

The British were very impressed. It made them realize that the Arabs really were strong enough to help them defeat the Turks. After this, the Arab Revolt worked much more closely with British forces, pushing northwards under the direction of the British Commander-in-Chief, General Edmund Allenby. The British army advanced north through Palestine, and Jerusalem was captured in December 1917. The Arabs played a vital role throughout, by constantly disrupting the railway further east, so distracting the Turks from the main British offensive, and confusing them about their enemy's strength.

By now, Lawrence had two main roles. He was liaising constantly with Allenby and other British officers, demanding supplies and discussing strategies, but he was also deeply committed to guerrilla fighting with the Arabs. He loved the desert, especially areas such as Wadi Rumm, where the desert rock formations are some of the most awe-inspiring in the world. Later, he wrote evocative descriptions of this harsh but beautiful landscape.

But the reality of the war had little romance to it. Lawrence was undergoing physical hardships that stretched him to the limit. There were occasional camel charges, but Lawrence was only one of many British soldiers involved. And, although he was a famous leader, he was not always in the front line. In fact, the famous charge into Akaba happened without him – in the confusion, Lawrence shot his own camel in the head, and it crumpled, throwing him off.

As the campaign wore on, Lawrence himself began to feel weary and sickened. After one raid on a Turkish train, in which 70 Turks were killed, he wrote to a friend, "*This killing and killing of Turks is horrible… you charge in at the finish and find them all over the place in bits.*"

Moreover, the Turks had proved to be brutal, cruel fighters – and barbaric in their treatment of wounded enemies, sometimes burning them alive. As a result,

Lawrence of Arabia

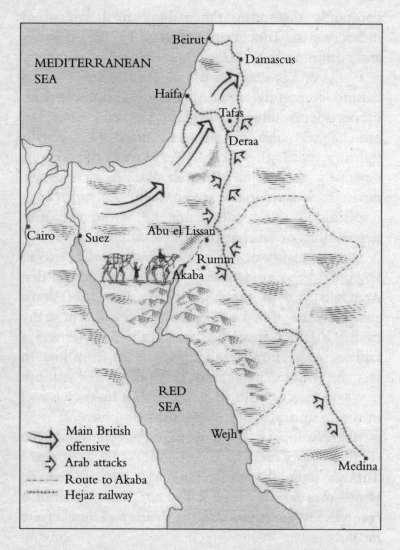

This map shows the Arabs' desert campaign and the route they took to Akaba.

the Arabs agreed among themselves to kill each other if they were too badly wounded to be carried away.

In April 1918, Lawrence himself had to put this rule into practice. On a reconnaissance mission behind enemy lines, one of his faithful servants, Farraj, was terribly wounded. As Lawrence and some other Arabs tried to carry him away, the alert was given – a group of Turks was approaching. There was nothing that could be done. Lawrence reached for his pistol, and pointed it at his friend's head.

"God will give you peace," muttered Farraj, as Lawrence pulled the trigger.

As 1918 wore on, at last it seemed that the British–Arab plan was working. After the successes of Akaba and Jerusalem, it had sometimes looked as though the campaign was stuck. But in September the Arabs succeeded in destroying the railway north and south of Deraa, one of the main lines of Turkish communication; and, in the same month, the British offensive wiped out the 7th and 8th Turkish armies in Palestine.

It was now just a case of trapping the remaining Turkish armies before they could retreat to Damascus. On September 26, 1918, Lawrence received news that two Turkish divisions were heading north in his direction, one of six thousand and the other of two thousand men. He and his fellow leaders decided they had enough men to tackle the smaller division.

They met the Turks just north of the village of Tafas, near Deraa, forcing them to turn back, and following them through the village of Tafas itself. What they saw appalled them. The Turks had massacred all the women and children; Lawrence himself noticed a pregnant woman who had been impaled on a bayonet.

The sheikh of the village, a warrior named Talal, was fighting alongside Lawrence. When he saw what had happened to his villagers, he gave a howl of grief and charged the retreating Turks on his own, only to be brought down in a shower of machine-gun bullets. But the whole Arab army was now enraged. Lawrence and the other leaders were so sickened that they gave the order to "take no prisoners" – which meant to kill all the Turks, whether they surrendered or not.

The Arabs swooped upon the Turks in fury at what they had done, and as a result soon captured Deraa. Then they went wild, looting and slaughtering Turks in vengeance for the massacre of Tafas. Lawrence later described it as "one of the nights in which mankind went crazy".

Meanwhile, the rest of the Arab army had taken on the larger Turkish divisions. In a few days, about five thousand Turks were killed, and eight thousand taken prisoner. Damascus was, at last, there for the taking.

The British allowed the Arab armies to march into Damascus ahead of them, in acknowledgement of their rights to the region. Lawrence went in with them, and witnessed the ecstatic welcome they were given by the people. Sherif Hussein was proclaimed King of the Arabs, and Feisal entered the city in triumph as his representative. For a short while it looked as though the Sykes–Picot agreement would be forgotten.

After hastily helping the Arab chiefs to establish order in Damascus, Lawrence left as soon as he could. Already, he seemed depressed. He knew that the Arabs' position was precarious, and that, in one sense, Feisal's struggle had only just begun. Exhausted, he headed home for London only four days later.

Sure enough, French demands quickly wiped out Feisal's dreams. By the end of 1920, the peace settlements had handed Lebanon and Syria over to France. To pacify the Arabs, Britain made Feisal king of Iraq under their indirect control; they gave an area known as Trans-Jordan (modern Jordan) to his brother Abdullah, under a similar arrangement. The only area ruled directly by Arabs remained Arabia itself, where Hussein was quickly toppled from power by a local rival, Ibn Saud, whose family gave its name to Saudi Arabia.

Afterwards

Lawrence played an important part in the post-war negotiations, fighting for the Arab right to independence. Although the eventual outcome was better than he feared, it was very different from the vision that had fired the Arab Revolt. It is clear that he felt the British had betrayed the Arabs; he was offered many distinctions and medals for his military service, including the Distinguished Service Order, but he turned them all down. Much to many people's disappointment, he began to retreat from the limelight.

But the legend of 'Lawrence of Arabia' began to grow, largely thanks to the journalist and public speaker Lovell Thomas, who went on a series of morale-raising tours. Lawrence himself regarded it as absurd that he had been singled out. Many other British officers had been involved in the Revolt, and he himself had certainly never been the leader of the Arabs. He claimed that Lovell Thomas was telling "red-hot lies".

Nevertheless, Lawrence began to write his own account of the Revolt, *Seven Pillars of Wisdom*. This made its own contribution to the legend, and some historians have claimed that it twists and exaggerates the facts. It contains many romantic descriptions of the desert, an idealized view of the Emir Feisal, and dramatic accounts of the battles. It also plays down the role of the British in defeating the Turks. As a result, the debate about Lawrence has gone on and on, and he still remains an enigmatic figure.

It has recently come to light that, in 1934, Lawrence was approached by the famous film director Alexander Korda, who wanted to make a film called *Lawrence of Arabia*. Lawrence was furious. "*Presumably he means me, and I have strong views as to the undesirability of any such film. So I have sent him word that perhaps he ought to discuss his intentions with me before he opens his silly mouth again,*" he wrote.

But the idea persisted. In 1962, 27 years after Lawrence's death, another film director, David Lean, did make a film called *Lawrence of Arabia*, starring Peter O'Toole as Lawrence. It quickly became a film classic, and ensured that the romantic image of war in the desert, with its heroism, flowing silk robes and charging camels, lived on to capture the imagination of millions.

T. E. Lawrence stayed in the RAF until 1935, when he was 46 years old. Only three months after leaving the service, he was killed in a motorcycle accident near his home in Dorset.

The legend of Zerzura

Somewhere, hidden away in the endless sands of the Libyan Desert, it was said that there was a beautiful lost oasis, where the palm trees were tall and lush, and where birds sang in their branches. There, in the white-walled ruins of an ancient city, a king and queen lay in an enchanted sleep from which one day, they would awake...

The name of this oasis was Zerzura, 'The Oasis of the Little Birds'. An Englishman and a Hungarian sat discussing it one day.

"You don't really believe in it, do you?" queried Dr. Richard Bermann, with an amused smile.

The Hungarian, Count Ladislaus Almasy, squinted against the sun, and shook his head impatiently. "The ancient city? Of course not. It's an old Arab myth from the *Kitab el Kanuz* – '*The Book of Hidden Treasures*'. But people have talked about Zerzura for hundreds of years. It's mentioned as far back as the 13th century. Even so, I'd think it was all nonsense if it wasn't for Wilkinson."

"Wilkinson?" Dr. Bermann looked at his friend curiously.

"Sir Gardiner Wilkinson. He was the chap who

first discovered Dakhla oasis," explained Almasy. "The locals told him about three oases out towards Kufra. They've since been found. They also told him about three other wadis [dry riverbeds], on the road to Farafra. Claimed there were palms, springs, ruins, just as the legends described. Zerzura…" Almasy's eyes grew pensive as he gazed into the distance. "Now if the people of Dakhla were right about the Kufra oases, why shouldn't they be right about Zerzura?"

Dr. Bermann nodded. It was difficult to disagree with Almasy when he was convinced of something. He was passionate about everything he did, but above all he was passionate about the desert – and the legend of Zerzura had fascinated him for years.

This map shows the region explored by Almasy.

The legend of Zerzura

Almasy was not alone in his love of the Libyan Desert (also known as the Western Desert), the vast expanse of the Sahara that stretches from eastern Libya to the river Nile in Egypt. Many others had been drawn to it before him. In 1879, German explorer Gerhard Rohlfs had crossed it from the east. He had reached the Kufra oasis in Libya, but had nearly lost his life along the way. Both he and his camels had been close to dying of thirst when a freak shower of rain fell, saving them. He named the spot Regenfeld (Rainfield), and ever after this it was a tradition for voyagers to stop and place a bottle there, containing details of their journeys.

Then, in the 1920s, a whole succession of explorers began to zigzag their way across the desert. One was a wealthy Egyptian, Sir Ahmed Hassanein Bey. He found two lost oases, Arkenu and Uweinat – but not Zerzura. Another Egyptian, Prince Kemal el Din, pioneered exploration in caterpillar vehicles, while an Englishman, Major R. A. Bagnold, hunted for Zerzura by car. But none of them found it. The oasis remained elusive.

Now, it was the early 1930s, and Almasy was one of the most single-minded explorers in the region. In 1932, he organized an expedition to find the oasis once and for all. He was joined by three Englishmen – Sir Robert Clayton-East-Clayton, Wing Commander H. Penderel and a cartographer (map maker) named Patrick Clayton – and six Egyptians.

They decided that they would hunt for the oasis by car, and make additional surveys from a Gypsy Moth plane named *Rupert*.

The main party set off from the Kharga oasis in Egypt on April 12, 1932 and headed for the Gilf Kebir, a vast mountain plateau in the south-east corner of the country. It was here, Almasy was sure, that they would find the lost oasis.

In the 1930s, desert exploration had come a long way, but it still had its fair share of dangers and excitements. Desert explorers had to keep their wits about them and look after each other; this was not the place to develop petty disagreements. The four Europeans worked together and, if they disliked each other, they did their best not to show it, at least at the time.

Taking turns flying *Rupert*, the Gypsy Moth, they weathered sandstorms and thirst to reach the Gilf Kebir, where the real exploration would begin. As they drew nearer, they realized they were running out of water. There was a fairly easy solution to this; they were within striking distance of Kufra, an oasis in Libya.

"We should go to Kufra for water before we carry on," said Almasy. "It won't take long."

"Kufra's in Italian territory," objected Patrick Clayton. "We can't go there. They'll arrest us."

"Don't be absurd," retorted Almasy. "Why on earth would they do that?"

"Because they don't like the British stamping on their territory, that's why!" snapped Clayton, who was well known for his dislike of the Italians.

"I'm not British," pointed out Almasy.

"No. You're not," said Clayton, in a strained tone of voice. The two men stared at each other. It was a strange moment. Perhaps it was a sign that the carefree days of desert exploration were coming to an end. The desert was no longer free of boundaries; no longer a hiding-place for legends... With the possibility of war looming, explorers were beginning to think about loyalties. Exploration meant information – as all the men knew only too well.

"What do you think, Penderel?" asked Almasy eventually.

The Wing Commander shrugged. "You're probably right," he said to Almasy. "They'll welcome you readily enough. But I'm a British soldier. If you want to go, you'd better go alone."

So Almasy headed west, leaving the rest of the team to make the first forays into the Gilf itself. The Italians gave him a warm welcome. He quickly stocked up on water and headed into the desert once more – but not before taking a number of interesting photographs.

In his absence, Sir Robert and Penderel flew the Gypsy Moth over the Gilf Kebir. To their great excitement, they spotted a long wadi in which many acacia trees were growing. Could this be the first of the three wadis spoken of by Wilkinson? When Almasy got back to camp and heard the news, he was just as excited. He was convinced that they had found Zerzura. Now the task remained of reaching the wadi by car.

But although the men flew over the enticing wadi several times, they were unable to find a way around to its entrance in their cars – the mountainous desert terrain of the Gilf Kebir blocked their way. They did find another wadi, but it was small and insignificant compared to the one they had seen from the air. And they were running out of time. Frustrated, they had to turn back.

The expedition party reached Cairo again in May 1932. In September that same year, tragedy struck. Sir Robert Clayton-East-Clayton contracted an acute viral infection. Within days, he was dead. He was only 24 when he died.

His wife, Lady Dorothy, was an intrepid woman who was determined to complete the exploration that her husband had begun. She discussed her options with Patrick Clayton in Cairo. The obvious thing to do would be to join up with her husband's former companions, including Almasy; but suddenly, Clayton's personal dislike of Almasy seemed to get the better of him. He knew how much Almasy wanted to continue the hunt for Zerzura, but he was out of the country at the time.

"Almasy won't be coming back to Cairo," Clayton

lied. "But I'm going on another expedition myself. I would be more than pleased for you to join me."

Lady Dorothy was delighted. "I shall certainly come with you," she told him. "I wouldn't want to travel in Almasy's company, anyway. Horrid man."

Lady Dorothy didn't like Almasy either, because she thought he was untrustworthy. More than once, she had refused to shake his hand on social occasions in Cairo. When Almasy returned to Egypt – as Clayton knew he would – he met her, and she treated him very coldly. He learned of her plans to follow up the Zerzura expedition with Clayton. He was furious, and hurriedly made plans of his own.

So it was that two expeditions, fired partly by rivalry, set out in 1933 to hunt for the missing wadis of Zerzura. This time, Almasy's expedition included his old friend Dr. Richard Bermann, a journalist who was very interested in the old legends, having discussed them with Almasy many times. They set out from Cairo on March 14, 1933, in four cars.

Their first stop was at a place called Abu Ballas, which means 'Father of Jars'. Here, hidden in the sand, were about three hundred water pots. They had been found by the people of Dakhla in the 19th century, when chasing off a gang of desert robbers. The pots obviously belonged to these robbers, who used them as a water supply point in their raids across the desert.

Excitedly, Almasy laid out a map.

"See here, Bermann," he said to his friend. "These jars are situated about two-thirds of the way between Kufra and Dakhla. That suggests that anyone trekking across the desert would have needed to stop for water somewhere else, as well – about one-third of the way between the two oases."

Almasy's finger traced the old caravan route with his finger. He let it hover over the Gilf Kebir.

"The Gilf Kebir... Zerzura?" asked Bermann, with a smile.

"Why not?" responded Almasy.

They left Abu Ballas and headed for the east side of the Gilf Kebir, hoping to find an entrance to the wadi they had seen the previous year. They drew a blank – but not before making another very useful discovery. Everyone had always thought there was no way through the Gilf Kebir. But they'd been wrong. The vast plateau was actually divided in two – there was a gap in the middle running from east to west. This was not a wadi, but an enormous rift in the rocks, through which their cars could pass easily.

"Very interesting," muttered Almasy. "Very useful, indeed."

Using this new discovery, they drove west to Kufra to stock up on supplies. There, they heard news of the other expedition. Patrick Clayton and Lady Dorothy had discovered the entrance to the wadi in the Gilf Kebir and, now satisfied, had headed back to Cairo.

"We'll follow their tracks into the wadi,"

announced Almasy immediately. "Then we'll go one better — once we're there, there might be clues about the other two wadis. But before we go, I'm going to talk to the locals."

Almasy was sure that the people of Kufra must know about the wadis hidden in the Gilf. Getting them to admit to it was another matter. The desert people did not like to give up their secrets to strangers. Eventually, he found an old caravan guide named Ibrahim who was willing to talk.

"This wadi you are talking about is called Wadi Abd el Melik," he told Almasy in strange, strongly accented Arabic. "There is another nearby. We call it Wadi Talh."

After a little persuasion, Ibrahim described how to reach the second wadi. But he refused to say whether there was a third. Satisfied for the time being, the expedition party set off once more.

"Wadi Abd el Melik and Wadi Talh," mused Almasy, as they drove along. "Only two. Is old Ibrahim telling the truth, do you think?"

They wound their way through the Gilf and, following the tracks of the Clayton expedition, eventually made their way into the Wadi Abd el Melik. It was long, and studded with acacia trees, but there was little else to say about it. All the other vegetation was dry and withered; there were two small rock springs, but they were almost dry. It was hardly a vision of paradise.

But Almasy was still determined to find Wadi Talh. With one of the Arab men, he drove the treacherous route to the top of the Gilf plateau and followed old Ibrahim's directions. Soon, sure enough, he came upon another wadi filled with acacia trees.

Jubilant, he returned to camp. Only one wadi remained to be found. Feeling pleased with themselves, the party headed for the oasis of Uweinat – where, once again, they bumped into Ibrahim. This time, the old man unbent a little further. When he heard of their discoveries, he admitted that there was indeed a third wadi, called Wadi Hamra – the Red Wadi. All three wadis were used by local herdsmen for grazing after the occasional rains. When it didn't rain for a long time, the vegetation disappeared.

So… Zerzura, or not? These poor wadis were hardly the stuff of legends – even the irrepressible Almasy had to admit that. The legend of Zerzura seemed like a mirage that was disappearing before their eyes. But it didn't matter too much; they had mapped out the area and had made some important navigational discoveries. And in those times of change, what was more important – a legend, or some well-drawn maps?

The party rested at Uweinat, and explored their surroundings. Almasy, who always tended to go further than everyone else, soon found something extraordinary. High up in the cliffs was a series of small caves containing prehistoric rock paintings in beautiful hues. They showed domesticated animals, especially cattle, and warriors carrying bows.

These were not the first paintings to be found in the area. In the 1920s, when Sir Ahmed Hassanein Bey had discovered Uweinat, he was told by a local nomad that djinns (spirits) had once lived in Uweinat, and had left their drawings on the rocks. Hassanein immediately sought out the pictures, and found they showed lions, giraffes, ostriches, different kinds of gazelles, and perhaps cows. He had pondered the fact that this region must have been much more fertile in ancient times and populated by many people, who had led a life of relative plenty.

Patrick Clayton had also discovered caves near the Gilf Kebir, which contained pictures of many giraffes, and also some lions. But it was Almasy's determined foraging that brought yet more of these caves to light. He and his team made photographic records, and Almasy himself made some sketches.

But the season had once more come to an end. The expedition packed up and headed back to Cairo. There, they heard that Patrick Clayton's party had made no further discoveries; but it had driven back from the Gilf right through the middle of the Great Sand Sea – the vast area of dunes that had almost killed Gerhard Rohlfs half a century before – which was a great achievement in itself.

When the summer heat was over, Almasy returned to Uweinat once again. On this occasion, he discovered the now-famous Cave of the Swimmers, in a rugged valley leading from Uweinat towards the Gilf Kebir. There, more paintings were found, which clearly showed people swimming. It offered final proof of how fertile this region had been in the old days. There must even have been a lake. Perhaps this, and not the three wadis, had given rise to the ancient legends of Zerzura – but who could really say?

Zerzura had once again eluded discovery and, as Europe drew closer to war, explorers had to turn their minds to other things. They could no longer be neutral. Their knowledge was too valuable, and the maps they made took on a new significance.

For most, there was no question as to whose side they were on. National loyalties ran very deep. But as a Hungarian, Almasy presented a mystery. Whose side was he on? The Hungarian government was sympathetic to Hitler and fascism, but it didn't follow that Almasy was himself a Nazi. He had acted inconsistently during his desert expeditions. In 1932, on the first Zerzura trip, he had taken photographs of the Italian military headquarters in Kufra oasis, and handed them to his British colleagues. Then, in 1933, he had revealed to the Italians in Kufra the east-west route through the Gilf Kebir.

A strange division of loyalties? Perhaps. But he had to come down on one side or the other – and eventually did so in style. He joined the German airforce, the Luftwaffe, as a desert adviser. By 1941,

The legend of Zerzura

German counter-intelligence, the Abwehr, was becoming very frustrated, because it couldn't seem to get any spies behind British lines and into Cairo. Almasy, spotting an opportunity to use his knowledge, stepped into the breach.

"I can get two German agents into Cairo for you," he told the Abwehr. "I will take them through Libya, via Kufra, and through the Gilf Kebir to Kharga, and from there to Assyut on the Nile."

At first, the Abwehr scoffed. But so far, all their other attempts had failed; and if anyone could get behind British lines, it was Almasy. They gave him the go-ahead, and the daring *Operation Salaam*, as it was called, was launched.

Almasy's first priority was his vehicles. In Tripoli, Libya's capital, two captured British Fords were given a thorough overhaul, and prepared for their long drive through the desert. Three trucks were to go with them, carrying supplies. Then Almasy met the German spies, agents Eppler and Sanstedte. In early 1942, *Operation Salaam* was ready, and the men set off.

It was Almasy's knowledge of the Gilf Kebir that made the mission a success. The trucks had no problems traversing the east-west gap that he had discovered nine years before. Eppler and Sandstedte were delivered safely to Assyut on May 24, 1942, after an incredible 3,200km (2,000-mile) drive.

Almasy's trip was one of the most daring

intelligence exploits of the Germans' desert campaign; although as it happens, they made little use of it. Shortly after the spies' arrival in Cairo, the British managed to catch the wireless operators who would have deciphered their messages. And, foolishly, the agents themselves squandered money in Cairo and threw lavish parties. It was not exactly difficult for the British to keep an eye on them.

Almasy himself disappeared back into the desert, and successfully made his way behind the Italian-German lines. The British had little chance of catching him; his long-time quest for Zerzura had made him as elusive as the legendary oasis itself...

Afterwards

Almasy survived the war, and wrote a number of books about his adventures in the desert. He died in Salzburg in 1951. Upon his grave is the Arabic epitaph *Abu Raml*, or 'Father of the Sands'.

If you have read Michael Ondaatje's novel *The English Patient*, or seen the film, some of this story may seem familiar to you. The novelist did use this extraordinary adventurer's life as material, although he changed many of the details. Katherine Clifton, Almasy's lover in Ondaatje's story, has no equivalent in reality. Some people have suggested that she was based on Lady Dorothy Clayton-East-Clayton, Sir

Robert's widow; but Lady Dorothy's dislike of Almasy seems to have been very real, and he was in any case alleged to be homosexual. Like her husband, Lady Dorothy met with a tragic end – in 1933, she was killed in a plane crash.

The oasis of Zerzura remains to be found.

Naming a desert

The landscape was desolate as far as the eye could see. To the west, there were never-ending red sandhills, rolling away into the distance. To the north-west, the land was flatter, but just as monotonous. There was nothing of interest to be seen to the south. Sweeping the scene with his binoculars, the only notable feature that the explorer could see lay to the north-east. There, in the far distance, through the shimmering haze, Ernest Giles saw a mountain.

He studied it carefully. "There are ridges running all the way down it," he informed his companion, lowering his binoculars. "That suggests water. I estimate it's about 50 miles [80km] away. That's where we're heading next."

William Tietkens, the man at his side, nodded in agreement. He didn't have much choice – Ernest Giles was the undisputed leader of the expedition. Along with just two other men, he had joined Giles in his dogged attempts to cross western Australia.

It was January 1874. Australia presented a great challenge to British explorers, who wanted to stake their claim to this vast 'uncivilized' land. Most had little respect for the people already living there, the Aboriginal people who knew the land intimately.

Instead, they saw it as their duty to reach the furthest corners of their new territory as quickly as possible, simply fighting off the Aboriginals along the way. As they went, they named each feature of the landscape – as though no one had ever seen it before.

In 1862, John McDouall Stuart had been the first white man to cross the continent from north to south. By 1872, a massive telegraph line had been built along his route. Now, the challenge was to cross Australia from the telegraph line to the west coast. Much of this land was desert.

The race was on. Ernest Giles made his first attempt in 1872. He got as far as the MacDonnell mountains, but then ran out of water and was forced to turn back. He decided to try again the next year. But by this time, two other explorers were in the race as well. Their names were Peter Warburton and William Gosse. Determined to beat them both, Ernest Giles set off on August 4, 1873.

By January 1874, Giles had reached mountains that he named the Rawlinson Range. He explored the area, and set up a base camp named Fort McKellar. To his disappointment, the mountains petered out. Beyond them, to the west, it seemed that there was nothing but more desert.

This was when he spied the mountain to the north-east with his companion William Tietkens. The two men returned to their camp and told the others – a young man named Jemmy Andrews, who was barely 20, and Alfred Gibson, who was slightly older. On February 1, 1874, the four men and over 20 horses set off for the tantalizing mountain.

It was a big mistake. Giles' estimation of the distance was not far wrong, but his other guess – that they would find water – was sadly mistaken. The horses were tired, and there was no water for them on the way. On top of this, it was the middle of summer, and the heat was blistering.

As soon as they found that the mountain was dry, Giles realized they had to get back to the Rawlinson Range as fast as they could. They walked by night, when it was cooler. But, even so, the trek proved too much for some of the horses. By the time they got back to Fort McKellar, four had died of thirst and exhaustion.

"Mount Destruction – that's the best name for this place," he announced in frustration.

So what could he do now? There seemed to be nothing but desert to the west. Knowing that others might already be ahead of him in the race, Giles desperately didn't want to admit defeat. While the horses recovered their strength, he considered his options.

Eventually, he decided to make a quick dash into the desert – just as far as they could go in a few days, to see what lay over the horizon. Perhaps the desert didn't stretch too far; he might find another source of water. This time, he wouldn't risk all the men and horses – he'd take just four horses and one other man. But which of the three should go with him?

The obvious choice was William or 'Mr.' Tietkens. He was very capable, and Giles referred to him by the title 'Mr.' because he was of the same social class as Giles himself. Taking Jemmy Andrews was out of the question. He was hard-working and willing, but young, uneducated and not very intelligent.

But the third man, Alfred Gibson, declared very strongly that he wanted to go with Giles. Like Andrews, Gibson was uneducated, but he was a little older, with a disagreeable, moody character. Giles didn't like him, and didn't really want to travel with him alone. He never washed, smelled very badly and he was always boasting. And although he had shown that he was quite good at taking on some responsibility, he could be careless. But Gibson insisted and, in the end, Giles gave in.

On April 20, they packed all they needed onto four horses. Two of the horses, a big bay cob and another horse named Darkie, were to carry enough supplies of dried horseflesh and water to last a week. Giles rode his best horse, the Fair Maid of Perth, while Gibson rode Badger, a steady horse with plenty of stamina. Off they set for the Circus, the last place in the Rawlinson Range that was known to have water. They spent the night there, and set off into the unknown early the next morning.

Gibson was in a cheerful mood that day. He chatted freely, much to Giles's surprise, for he was often sullen and sulky.

"How is it," he asked Giles, "that so many people on these sorts of expeditions go off and die?"

Giles considered his response. "Well, Gibson," he said thoughtfully, "there are many dangers involved in exploring – other than the risk of accidents, of course. But I would say that most people die through lack of judgement, or knowledge, or courage. Then again, of course, we all have to die, sooner or later."

"Well, I wouldn't like to die in this part of the country," said Gibson.

"Nor I!" agreed Giles.

They rode along in silence after this, through a landscape of sandhills covered in spinifex, the most common plant of the western deserts. After a few hours they stopped and allowed the horses to rest.

The men were very hungry by this stage, so Giles unpacked some of the horseflesh from Darkie's back. What he found appalled him.

"Gibson!" he called. "I thought I told you to pack enough horseflesh for a week."

Gibson looked at him sullenly. "I did," he said defiantly.

"There is barely enough to feed one man here," said Giles angrily. "And certainly not two."

He had given the job of packing the meat to Gibson, and hadn't checked it since. Gibson was silent, and Giles sighed. There was no point in arguing over the issue; they would have to make do with what they had. They rested in the shade for a while, then set off again in the scorching afternoon heat. By nightfall, they had covered a good distance.

"40 miles [65km] in one day," said Giles, as they set up camp. "Not bad at all."

Giles slept badly. He had a horror of ants – which were everywhere – and found it amazing that his companions could sleep with them crawling all over them. This night was no exception. Gibson slept soundly.

At daybreak they set off again, and plodded for another 30km (20 miles) through a landscape that gradually changed – but only from one sort of desert to another. The sandhills gave way to gravel, then to larger stones. It was hard going on the horses' feet. Then, when they stopped to rest, Giles discovered that one of the water bags had leaked. They had not only less horseflesh to eat, but less water to drink, too.

"We had better get rid of the packhorses," said Giles. "We'll send them back. Then we shall have the remaining water for ourselves and the other horses."

Giles hoped that the horses would instinctively follow the tracks they had made on the way out, and slowly make their way to where there had last been water.

"Well, I'd rather ride the cob than Badger," said Gibson. "I'll send Badger and Darkie back."

Giles looked doubtful. "Gibson, I chose Badger for you because I know he can stay the course. He has stamina."

Gibson shook his head stubbornly. "I prefer the cob," he insisted. "He's fresh enough now."

"Yes," said Giles patiently. "But we haven't tested him to the limit. He might not be up to it. We only know what Badger and the Fair Maid of Perth are made of."

Gibson shrugged sullenly. "I want to ride the cob," he repeated.

Giles sighed in exasperation. Gibson really was impossible sometimes. "Very well," he said. They needed to make up their minds, and send the horses on their way. "You shall ride the cob."

It was a fateful decision. Giles might well have remembered his own words at this point – that people met their deaths in the desert through lack of judgement, knowledge, or courage... a serious error of judgement had just been made.

At this spot, they left some kegs of water, which would be much needed on their return. They rested until the heat began to die down, then set off again and managed another 30km (20 miles). There was still no sign of an end to the desert. It stretched in all directions, to the horizon and beyond.

That night they tried to sleep, but their two remaining horses gave them little rest. The desperate creatures nosed around for the waterbags, craving a drink. Giles had hung their last few pints in a tree, and smelling it, the Fair Maid of Perth marched up to the bag and grasped it between her teeth. As she

89

pulled at it, the stopper flew out, and a jet of water shot into the air and splattered on the ground. Giles and Gibson stared at it in disbelief, their throats dry and choking. They now had only about a pint of water left between them.

The cob was even more desperate than the mare. He nosed around the camp frantically, looking for water. Gibson stared at the wretched animal with resentment.

"I wish I'd stuck to Badger," he announced. "The cob's been getting slower all afternoon. Funny. He was always game before."

Giles said nothing. What could he say, after all?

They started out again before daybreak, and trudged another 15km (10 miles). There, they saw some ridges up ahead – a change in the landscape, at last! A little further on, things were definitely looking hopeful. There was a range of mountains in the distance, about a day's journey away. Giles gazed at them longingly, but they had come 160km (98 miles) from the last water. And things were not going well.

"Giles!" called Gibson, who was riding behind him. "I think the cob is dying."

Giles looked back and stared at the sorry creature in dismay. The cob's head was hanging low, and he could barely put one foot in front of another. There was no doubt about it – they had to turn back. Immediately.

"I name those mountains the Alfred and Marie

range," said Giles, with one final, regretful glance in their direction. "After the Duke and Duchess of Edinburgh. I hope, please God, I shall one day set foot there."

But the plight of the cob was terrible. He had not gone far when he stopped in his tracks.

"I'll get off," said Gibson. "We'll have to drive him forward instead."

The cob dragged himself a little further, but then his legs collapsed beneath him. He lay down, his eyes dull and glassy. It was clear that he was never going to rise again.

The men were now in a dreadful situation. Two men and one horse – all exhausted and with barely

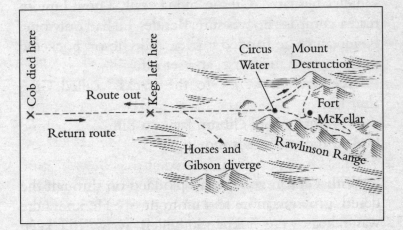

This map shows the trip to Mount Destruction, and Giles and Gibson's route into the desert.

any water. Giles dismounted, and allowed Gibson to ride the Fair Maid of Perth while he walked. It was tough going. After an hour or two they stopped, and gulped down the last of their water. Giles had been thinking hard.

"Gibson," he said, "we can't carry on like this. One of us must go ahead on the horse. I shall stay behind. Now, listen to me. Get to the kegs of water that we left, and give the mare a drink or she will die. Leave as much water as you can for me, then carry on. Stick to the tracks we've made, and don't leave them. When you reach camp, send Mr. Tietkens with water and fresh horses. I will follow, and get as far as I can on foot."

"Very well," said Gibson. "But I'd be better off if I had a compass."

Giles hesitated. Gibson didn't really know how to read a compass, he was sure. Besides, he had only one. Reluctantly, he handed it over, and Gibson pocketed it. He turned the horse, and set off.

"Remember – stick to the tracks!" called Giles after him.

"Alright," called Gibson back to him.

And then he was gone.

With Gibson gone, Giles plodded on through the desert, growing more and more thirsty. He knew the water kegs were 50km (30 miles) away. "If I keep going, I'll reach them tomorrow afternoon," he said to himself.

With sheer effort and determination, he reached the kegs the next day. Gibson had been and gone, leaving him two and a half gallons of water, and a few sticks of smoked horseflesh. Giles was ravenous, and choking with thirst, but he knew he had to ration himself carefully. He sat down and thought the situation through. He was 100km (60 miles) from the Circus, and 130km (80 miles) from camp. It would take at least six days for anyone to get back to him. Should he just sit and wait, or keep on going? Walking further would mean carrying the water keg, which was very heavy and cumbersome. It was a terrible dilemma.

"After I had thoroughly digested all points of my situation, I concluded that if I did not help myself Providence wouldn't help me either," wrote Giles later. Shouldering the heavy water keg, he staggered forward, following the tracks – as he had told Gibson to do.

The next few days passed in a blur. Giles could only walk very slowly, because of the heat and the weight of the keg. 25km (15 miles) beyond the kegs, he stopped.

"That's funny," he muttered to himself.

The main line of horse tracks carried on in front of him, but the tracks of the two horses they had set free now wandered off to the south. And, as he studied these tracks carefully, Giles' heart sank. Instead of following the main line of tracks, it was

93

clear that Gibson had followed the loose horses.

"Perhaps they will all return to the main line soon," thought Giles. He staggered on, looking anxiously all the time for Gibson's tracks, in the hope that he had realized his mistake and come back. But there was never any sign of him.

Giles plodded doggedly on, growing weaker and weaker. Whenever he sat down to rest, his head would swim when he tried to rise again. He fell over many times, but forced himself to keep on going. When he finished the last of his water, he was still 30km (20 miles) from the Circus. But, now that he could dump the heavy keg, he made one last enormous effort. He reached the Circus at daybreak, after a long night's walking. It was a whole week since Gibson had left him.

Giles sat down at the waterhole, and drank and drank. There were now only 30 km (20 miles) between himself and camp, where at last he would find some food. But he was so desperate that he resorted to other means of feeding himself.

"*Just as I left the Circus,*" he wrote, "*I picked up a small dying wallaby, whose mother had thrown it from her pouch. It weighed about two ounces [60g], and was scarcely furnished yet with fur. The instant I saw it, like an eagle I pounced upon it and ate it raw, dying as it was, fur, skin, and all. The delicious taste of that creature I shall never forget.*"

Now out of serious danger, Giles made the final 30km (20 miles) and arrived at Fort McKellar at daybreak about two days later. He woke Mr. Tietkens, who stared at him as though he was a ghost.

"Give me – food," Giles croaked hoarsely.

Tietkens hurriedly did so. "Where's Gibson?" he asked, as soon as Giles could speak properly.

Giles shook his head, and they realized in horror that he must surely be dead by now. There had been no sign of him, either at the Circus waters or at the camp. Giles told Tietkens about his tracks, and how they had left the main line.

"We must go back and look for him," said Giles, although he could barely move. When he was strong enough, they loaded up the horses and launched a search. But, despite all their efforts, they found nothing at all.

Afterwards

With Gibson assumed dead, Giles was forced to end the expedition. He named the desert the Gibson Desert, in memory of his companion.

Sadly, the group retreated, and reached Charlotte Waters on July 13, 1874. There, Giles received bitterly disappointing news. Although his rival Gosse had been forced to turn back, Warburton had taken a more northerly route across what became known as the Great Sandy Desert. With camels instead of horses, he had succeeded where Giles had failed.

What was worse, another explorer named John

Forest had started out from Perth in the hope of crossing the desert from the west. He, too, had succeeded.

But Giles' exploring days were far from over. In 1875, he took a more southerly route, and reached the west coast via the Great Victoria Desert. Then, in 1876, he crossed back again, this time through the ill-fated Gibson Desert. He hoped to find some trace of his old companion; but, to this day, Gibson has never been found.

The Abode of Emptiness

In the southern half of Saudi Arabia lies a vast area of desert, so barren that even its name suggests a desolate place where nothing can survive. This name, in Arabic, is the *Rub'al Khali*, which translates as 'the Empty Quarter' – or, more poetically, 'the Abode of Emptiness'. Right up until the 1930s, no white man had ever ventured any distance into this wilderness of rock and sand; and certainly no one had ever crossed it.

But, as more and more of the world's areas of wilderness were reached by explorers, it seemed that there was little else to be conquered. The Rub'al Khali was one of the last great challenges – and there were two men who were determined to be the first to cross it.

Both of them were English. One was Harry St. John Philby, a close supporter of the Saudi king, Ibn Saud. He lived in Mecca, the holy city of Islam, and had become a Muslim, taking on the religion of his chosen country.

The other man, Bertram Sidney Thomas, had none of Philby's contacts in the Saudi royal court. He had the friendship of the Sultan of Muscat in Oman, but that wouldn't really help when it came to his desert adventure. If he was going to succeed, he would have to take care of himself.

For Philby, crossing the Rub'al Khali was an obsession that had consumed him for years. In 1924, he had been on the verge of making the expedition, but a revolution in Saudi Arabia had prevented him from setting off. He had then suffered a very bad bout of dysentery, and was forced to give up his plans. By 1930, with Ibn Saud safely on the throne, Philby was desperate to try again, and constantly pestered the king for permission and support.

Meanwhile, Thomas was going about things very differently. Between 1927 and 1930, he made a number of preparatory journeys by camel, in the area just south of the Rub'al Khali itself. He knew that he would have to win the trust of the local Bedouin tribes to make the crossing, because he had no intention of asking for the king's permission.

"I knew the mind of authority," he wrote, *"and so avoided the pitfall of seeking permission for my designs… So my plans were conceived in darkness, my journeys heralded only by my disappearances."* He immersed himself in Bedouin customs, dressing like them, speaking their language, and making sure he did nothing to offend them.

It was a shrewd policy. While Philby sat impatiently in Mecca waiting for the king to make his mind up, Thomas was putting together his final plans. In October 1930, he sailed from Muscat to the region of Dhufar, on the south coast of Saudi Arabia, where he had arranged for guides and camels from the Rashid, a Bedouin tribe, to meet him.

Philby heard of Thomas's arrival in Dhufar, and grew desperately impatient. The king knew how badly he wanted to go, so he consulted a local governor.

"Is such a trip wise, at this time?" he asked.

The governor said that the political situation was still unstable. "Wait another year," he advised.

There was nothing Philby could do. He was absolutely furious.

But for Thomas, things were not going smoothly either. On arrival in Dhufar, his camels and guides were nowhere to be found. It appeared that the Rashid tribesman he had negotiated with had simply pocketed the money that Thomas had given him, and disappeared back into the desert. Frustrated, Thomas sent out messengers to find him; meanwhile, he just had to wait.

Six weeks later, there was still no sign of his guides and camels. Thomas was on the verge of despair: the ship that had brought him from Muscat was now scheduled to return. Thomas thought he would have to give up his plans, board the ship and return unsatisfied to Muscat. Perhaps Philby would get his chance to beat him in the end.

But then, at the eleventh hour, about 40 Rashid

men appeared with the same number of camels. He could set off after all!

Thomas's route ran from the south of the Rub'al Khali, more or less in a straight line north-east. The main problem he faced was crossing the different tribal areas. The Rashid tribesmen of the south would not enter the feared Murra territory to the north. But, thanks to a great deal of patient negotiation, Thomas found a solution. He would travel in relays. When he reached Murra territory, a new set of camels and Murra tribesmen would meet him, and he would leave the Rashid tribesmen behind.

With this all arranged, Thomas set off. The going was very slow. Whenever there was good grazing – as there was in the early stages of the trip – his guides insisted on allowing the camels to feed, in case they did not come across any later.

This was one of the many desert practices that Thomas had to learn. Another was the Bedouin rule of hospitality. If strangers appear in a desert camp in need of food, they must never be turned away hungry. The knowledge that a rich foreigner was crossing the sands caused a number of such 'strangers' to appear. How on earth were his supplies going to last, Thomas wondered in frustration.

But the days of patient trekking passed by without any major problems. Thomas got along well with the tribesmen. At night, around the campfire, they told him their stories and legends, and he wrote them all down. Many were about an ancient tribe known as the Bani Hillal, and their hero, Abu Zaid. It was said that no spear or sword could kill him, because his mother was descended from a *djinn* (a spirit). Abu Zaid was also famous for his generosity – he had killed all his camels to feed to strangers…

Thomas listened, fascinated, immersed in this world of softly padding camels and never-ending landscapes. But by the time the group reached the waterhole of Shanna, where Murra guides were to take over, one of the camels was very sick. Its fate was brutal and swift. It was dragged into a shallow in the sand, and the men cut its throat, relishing the idea of meat instead of camel milk and oatmeal. Despite his hunger, Thomas was not quite so delighted. He found the meat tough and stringy, and could barely force it down. He watched in astonishment as the tribesmen enjoyed another desert delicacy – they slit open the camel's bladder, and drank her urine. Delicious! Or so they said – much better than the salty, bitter water of the waterholes.

Thomas set off again on January 10, 1931, with a smaller group of men and camels. This second leg of the journey was disrupted by sandstorms, which made life very miserable and wrecked some of Thomas's instruments. Added to this, it was bitterly cold, especially at night. "*Sand filled my eyes, and my notebooks,*" Thomas wrote; "*sand was everywhere; note-taking with numbed fingers was impossible, and all that could be done was to sit idly in the swirl of sand and cold discomfort..."*

But none of this was life-threatening. Thomas's troubles were minor, considering what could easily have happened. The warlike tribesmen remained peaceful, there was an ample supply of camels' milk, and Thomas remained in good health – as did everyone else, including the camels. In early February 1931, Thomas reached his destination of Doha, in present-day Qatar, on the Persian Gulf coast.

Thomas had done it! The news soon reached Mecca, and Philby took it very badly. He was so disappointed that he shut himself away for a week.

When he appeared in public again, he was full of fury about Thomas's achievement – fury mixed with scorn. "What's the point in marching in a straight line?" he stormed. "Thomas's journey was useless. He hasn't *explored* the Rub'al Khali. I'll show him how it's done."

But he was still waiting for the king's permission to set out. Months passed. Philby sat in Jeddah, depressed, disillusioned with the king and Saudi Arabia in general. Then, in December 1931, out of the blue, came the news he was longing for – he had permission at last, and the king's support. Philby was jubilant.

As soon as possible, he headed for his starting point: Hufuf, an inland town not far from Thomas's finishing point, Doha. Everything he needed was waiting for him: 32 camels, 14 men and provisions for three months. His journey could begin at last. Philby set off on January 7, 1932.

Heading in the opposite direction from Thomas, Philby was determined from the outset to cover more ground and make more discoveries. First of all, he wanted to find the ruins of a mythical city that a guide had once told him about. It was called Wabar, and was said to have been the home of a sinful king, Ad Ibn Kinad. To punish the king for his sinfulness, God had destroyed Wabar by fire.

Philby followed the guide's instructions and found the site quite easily. What he discovered, however, were not ancient ruins, but the craters left by a large shower of meteors. Fragments of iron and silica lay around the area, and Philby was careful to collect specimens. The mystery solved, he moved on.

But his journey soon took on a different character from Thomas's. Philby had not developed any personal trust with the Bedouin. They didn't understand why he insisted on taking a more difficult route than he needed to, or why he constantly made detours to fill in his maps. They also wanted to spend time hunting a desert antelope called the oryx, but Philby wouldn't let them. Unwillingly, they got as far as the waterhole of Shanna.

At Shanna, the disputes reached a new level. Philby wanted to take a completely new route to the west, while his guides wanted to follow the route taken by

Thomas. They couldn't see the point of heading into a wilderness with no known waterholes. Philby had to bribe them to continue by paying them in advance.

With tempers still simmering, the group set off again. But things didn't improve. After five days, when they were 230km (140 miles) into the desert, the disputes brought the group to a halt. The camels were at the point of collapse, and all the men were desperate with hunger; they had eaten nothing but dates since leaving Shanna. But Philby still refused to let them slow the expedition down by going off to hunt oryx. To make matters worse, he insisted on walking in the daytime, when it was hot, so that he could make all his observations.

A desert oryx

The men had had enough. Philby was forced to give way, and allow the group to turn back. He described this day as *"the worst of the whole journey from beginning to end, and perhaps the most terrible of all my experience"*. But turn back they did, towards the waterhole of Naifa, north of Shanna.

Now encouraged at the thought of water, the guides kept up a fast pace, and Philby had little choice in the matter. They stopped only to allow one of the camels to give birth – and the baby camel was killed immediately for food. The men made a small fire and tried to roast it, but they were so desperate they couldn't wait for it to cook. As they ate ravenously, it was still quite raw. *"I could have eaten anything, cooked or raw,"* wrote Philby later.

After four days of relentless marching, the men reached Naifa and drank its bitter water with relish. They slaughtered another camel for some much-needed meat, and rested. But now Philby had to decide what to do next. He was still determined to cross the desert to the west, as he had planned; but it was now clear that the baggage camels simply couldn't take the pace, and were slowing everything down. The only way to succeed would be to travel light, and fast. He decided to split the group up and send the heavy baggage back to Hufuf.

Now the men could choose whether or not to come with him on the tough journey that lay ahead – 560km (350 miles), with no certainty of water.

When they had rested, a surprising number said they would come. In the end, he sent only seven men back to Hufuf.

This part of the journey was particularly gruelling. Philby squabbled with the men over his rations. When they tried to shame him for not sharing his camel's milk, he refused to drink any more milk for the entire journey.

Choking with thirst, Philby stared out across a bleak gravel plain that contained nothing else whatsoever – not even thorny desert vegetation. Philby's guides, taking the matter into their own hands, decided that the best way to cross it was just to keep going. It was a fantastic feat of endurance – 110km (70 miles) of non-stop travel, with 18 out of 21 hours in the saddle.

But once they were over the plain, the guides began to recognize landmarks. They were nearing their destination, the oasis of Suleiyil on the north-west fringes of the Rub'al Khali. The hungry, thirsty men and their camels walked into the oasis on March 14, 1932.

Afterwards

So whose achievement was greater? Both Philby and Thomas wrote detailed accounts of their journeys, including maps, long lists of wildlife and

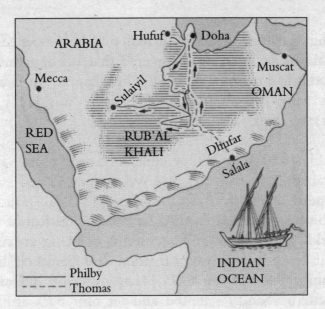

This map shows the routes taken by Philby and Thomas through the Rub'al Khali.

flora and geological features. It's difficult to say who contributed more knowledge of the region. Thomas indisputably made the first crossing, but Philby's route was the more difficult one.

Perhaps Thomas cheated by avoiding the issue of permission. Philby would certainly have won the race otherwise. But neither of the men could set out without the help and guidance of the Bedouin tribes, for whom the whole idea of a 'first crossing' was probably very strange. Thomas won their support through patient dealings, and kept their good will throughout – a great personal achievement in itself.

Philby, on the other hand, made his trip with the

king's protection. As it turned out, he'd needed it. Many years later, he discovered that his disgruntled guides had planned to kill him at Shanna, but fear of the king had stopped them. So he was lucky to survive at all.

Harry St. John Philby continued to explore Saudi Arabia for many years, and was acknowledged as an expert on both Arabian geography and politics. However, in his later years he became critical of the Saudi government and accused it of being corrupt. The government was offended and banished him from the country in 1955. He went to live in Beirut until the Saudis relented and let him back in. He returned, but didn't settle in Arabia again. He died in Beirut in September 1960.

Bertram Sidney Thomas also lived in the Middle East for much of his life. He held a number of important posts in Bahrain, Palestine and Lebanon. He died in Cairo in December 1950.

The vanished airman

If a human body is left in the sands of the Sahara, it doesn't rot away. Instead – as the ancient Egyptians knew very well – the intense, dry heat quickly sucks away all the moisture, and the skin turns to brittle leather. The body becomes a mummy.

In 1962, a French army patrol was driving through one of the most remote parts of the Sahara, south of the town of Reggan in Algeria. It is so remote that even the desert nomads rarely enter it, and call it Tanezrouft – 'the land of thirst'. So it was particularly surprising when someone suddenly spotted the glint of sunlight on metal, up ahead.

"What's that?" the men called to one another. They drove closer.

"Looks like a plane!"

It was indeed a plane, lying upside down in the sand, a total wreck. And underneath one of its wings, his body parched and mummified, lay the pilot. His name was Captain Bill Lancaster, and he had lain there undiscovered for a total of 29 years.

Carefully, the French patrol inspected the wrecked plane. It was an Avro Avian, a single-seater biplane of the kind used by aviation enthusiasts in the 1930s. Tied to a wing strut were the plane's documents, the logbook, Lancaster's passport and a wallet, all carefully wrapped in fabric to protect them. Lying nearby was a Shell fuel card with a final message:

"So the beginning of the eighth day has dawned. It is still cool. I have no water... I am waiting patiently. Come soon please. Fever wracked me last night..."

On opening the fragile logbook, the patrol found 41 pages detailing the pilot's last flight, his crash, and the terrible eight days that he spent hoping to be rescued, but instead dying slowing of thirst. His bravery in the face of death was astonishing – and said a great deal about a man who, only 12 months before, had been accused of murder...

Captain Bill Lancaster had led an eventful life. He was born in England in 1898, but emigrated to Australia during his teens. During the First World War he trained as a pilot, and joined the British Royal Air Force after the war. In 1927, the RAF no longer needed him, and he wondered what to do. He didn't want to give up flying; so when he had the idea of becoming the first man to fly from England to Australia, it seemed like the perfect way to make a name for himself as a pilot.

Things soon fell into place. He was offered an Avro Avian plane at a special price, and Shell offered to pay for his fuel. When he met an Australian woman who wanted to become the first woman to make the journey – and offered to find half the funds – the idea suddenly became a reality. The woman's name was Jessie Miller, 'Chubbie' to her friends.

The pair set off on October 14, 1927, from Croydon Airport near London. The flight turned into an adventure that lasted five months, as they struggled with bad weather conditions, mechanical failure and a crash-landing in Sumatra, Indonesia. When they finally arrived in Australia, hundreds of people were there to greet them. But only Chubbie had achieved her goal. She was the first woman to make the flight, but Bill just missed being the first man. Their flight had taken so long that another pilot, Bert Hinkler, had overtaken them on the way.

During their adventure, Bill Lancaster and Chubbie Miller fell in love, although both were already married. It was a love affair that would have devastating results.

Chubbie built on her fame by getting her own pilot's licence and entering flying competitions. She and Bill went to America, where she became well known in aviation circles. Then she had the idea of writing a book about her adventures, and she looked for a writer to help her. She found Haden Clarke, a handsome young man, who came to live with her and Bill in their house in Miami to work with Chubbie on the book.

For Bill, things were not working out quite so well. He consistently had problems finding work. In

1932, he was given the job of piloting a plane in Mexico. Unable to pick and choose, he set off, leaving Chubbie and Haden alone in the Miami house.

Chubbie was left alone with very little money, and she soon grew frustrated and bored. Stuck in the house with Haden, the charming writer soon captured her heart, and she even agreed to marry him. The pair both wrote to Bill to tell him the news, and he flew home from Mexico at once. He was distraught. He adored Chubbie, and couldn't believe that she had betrayed him so easily,

With the three of them staying in the house in Miami, it is hardly surprising that things reached a dramatic climax. On the night of April 20, 1932, Haden Clarke was shot in the head, and died soon afterwards in hospital. There were two suicide notes, but it didn't take the police long to decide that they were forgeries – and that Bill had written them. A week after Clarke's death, Bill Lancaster was arrested for his murder.

The trial was a big sensation. Everyone was sure that Lancaster must be guilty. Haden Clarke had been his rival – Lancaster had had an obvious reason and every opportunity to kill him. But Lancaster denied it. He insisted he was innocent. And, as the trial wore on, it began to seem that he might be telling the truth. It was clear that he was an honest, decent man, whereas evidence about Haden Clarke showed him to be unstable and a heavy drinker. He had even threatened suicide before.

The day of the verdict was desperately nerve-wracking for Lancaster. His whole life hinged on this moment… As the foreman of the jury intoned "Not guilty", the whole court rang out with applause from the people listening.

But, in fact, Lancaster's life was in ruins anyway. Finding work had been hard enough, but no one wanted to have anything to do with him after the trial, despite the verdict. What could he do? He and Chubbie headed to England, away from the glare of bad publicity. There, Lancaster pondered his future. He had no money. His flying career was in tatters. His only idea was to set another flying record, which might restore his reputation in aviation circles.

Lancaster's father, seeing that his son was desperate, agreed to fund the trip. Lancaster decided to go for the England–Cape Town record, which had recently been broken by the British pilot Amy Johnson. She had set a time of four days, six hours and 54 minutes. It was a tough challenge, and from the start, Lancaster didn't really think it through properly.

He chose for his plane another Avro Avian, this time a single-seater called the Avian Mk.V Southern Cross Minor. He was particularly fond of flying Avians, having flown to Australia in one; but it was still a rather foolish choice. Amy Johnson had made her flight in a De Havilland Puss Moth, which had a cruising speed of 37kph (20mph) faster than the Avian. To beat her record, Lancaster would have to make the flight almost non-stop – a physical feat of endurance that would test the strongest man.

But Lancaster was no longer strong. Both mentally and physically, he was exhausted from the ordeal of the previous year. Everything he said before the flight suggested that he was in no fit state to do it.

"I want to make it clear that I am attempting this at my own risk," he told a reporter. "I don't expect any efforts to be made to find me if I'm reported missing." They were hardly optimistic words – perhaps even fateful…

On the morning of April 11, 1933, Chubbie and Lancaster's parents came to see him off from Lympne Aerodrome, near the South Kent coast.

"Goodbye, darling," said his mother, handing him some chicken sandwiches and a bar of chocolate.

Lancaster embraced them all tightly, then climbed into the cockpit. He started the engine. It was 5:38am.

His first stop was supposed to be at Oran, in Algeria – a big hop from England of 1,770 km (1,100 miles). But from the word go, he had terrible luck. The winds were against him, and he had to land in Barcelona in Spain to refuel. He battled on to Oran, his nerves becoming frayed. He was already behind schedule. The officials at Oran looked concerned when they saw him. He was jittery and bad-tempered, and certainly in no condition to make the treacherous desert crossing.

"Monsieur, we really think you should reconsider," said one official. "You need to rest."

"Rest!" exploded Lancaster. "I'm already late. I can't rest. And you fellows are only slowing me down."

"It's in your own interest, monsieur," said the official patiently. "Crossing the desert is exhausting at the best of times. And I might remind you that we require a £100 deposit against our search costs, should we need to come and look for you."

"I've already paid my deposit!" exclaimed Lancaster – which was true. He had paid the sum in London.

"I'm afraid we have no record of that," said the official. "You will have to pay it again."

Lancaster was furious. "Well, I don't have £100!" he argued. "I'll take my chances, and I don't expect you to look for me."

With these words, he climbed back into his cockpit and taxied down the runway. The officials shook their heads. It was three o'clock in the morning. Lancaster had been on the go for nearly 24 hours.

The next leg of the journey took Lancaster over the Atlas Mountains and across the first stretch of desert. He flew on through the night, checking his compass by flashlight.

As dawn broke, he looked down from his cockpit anxiously, straining to catch sight of the trans-Sahara track that led down to the town of Reggan, his next scheduled stopping point. To his relief, there it was, stretching southwards across the arid wastes. He decided to stop at Adrar, 160km (100 miles) north of Reggan, then skip Reggan altogether and get the desert over with in one mammoth flight.

But Lancaster's exhaustion was getting the better of him. He took off from Adrar at about half past nine in the morning, and immediately lost his way. Below him, a sandstorm was raging, which obscured the track heading south. Instead, he headed east. This was disastrous. He flew on for over an hour and a half before realizing what he had done. He then landed at a small place called Aoulef to check exactly where he was. Eventually, he headed south to Reggan – but he had lost hours of valuable time and was running out of fuel. He would have to land at Reggan after all.

Did Lancaster know that this stop would be his last contact with the world? It almost seems as though he had a death wish. He landed at Reggan and clambered out of the cockpit. He had not eaten or slept for 30 hours, and his condition alarmed officials.

"Look at him! He can hardly walk," commented one, as Lancaster staggered towards them.

"We can't let him carry on," agreed another. "He's a danger to himself."

The officials, like those at Oran, did everything in

their power to stop him from continuing. But Lancaster was as determined as ever. Passing a hand over his face in exhaustion, he was very clear about his intentions.

"I'm carrying on," he told them. "This is my only chance. My only chance, do you hear me? I am not going to fail. I cannot fail."

Impressed with his courage, one official tried to reason with him more gently. "But you are already 10 hours behind schedule," he said. "You are exhausted. It would not be in any way disgraceful to give up now. Better to fail than to die in the desert."

But the look in Lancaster's eyes revealed that failure was his biggest fear of all.

The man sighed, and relented. "I can't stop you from going," he admitted. "And of course, we can't ignore you if you don't arrive. If we don't hear anything by six o'clock tomorrow, I will send a search car down the track to Gao. If you can burn something to light a beacon, we should see you."

So, at eight o'clock that evening, Lancaster once more climbed slowly into the cockpit. The officials watched him with heavy hearts as the plane weaved and wobbled down the runway. It was clear that Lancaster could barely concentrate on the controls. The plane lurched into the sky.

But as they watched, the Avian swung around smoothly enough, and began to fly south. Lancaster was on his way again – but his chances of survival were looking slim…

The vanished airman

Up above the Sahara, Lancaster knew he had 800km (500 miles) of desert ahead of him. If he could just stay awake, and keep to the trans-Saharan track, all would be well... He was staring intently at his cockpit controls when the engine gave a cough. Lancaster's heart started pounding. He checked all his controls, but could find nothing wrong. Then the engine coughed again – and again...

The plane started to drop. Lancaster fought with the controls, but there was nothing he could do. He was coming down. It was dark, and he couldn't judge his distance from the ground. He tried to guess, but it was hopeless.

There was a sickening crunch as the plane crashed into the desert sands and turned over. Lancaster knew no more. Everything went black...

This map shows Lancaster's flight path and the site of the crash.

When he came around, Lancaster could see nothing. He wondered where he was, and what had happened to him. Had he gone blind? He seemed to be upside down, and the air was heavy with fumes. He put a hand to his eyes, and realized they were clogged with congealed blood. He rubbed them until they opened.

Now, he could assess his situation. He was indeed upside down in the tiny cockpit, which was spattered with blood. He felt his face carefully. There were deep cuts on his forehead and nose, but at least they had stopped bleeding now. How long had he been unconscious? He had no idea, but he could tell he had lost a lot of blood. He felt weak and faint. He scrabbled around and managed to heave himself out of the cockpit.

"*I have just escaped a most unpleasant death,*" he wrote in his logbook. It did not seem to occur to him that an even more unpleasant one lay ahead. He checked his supplies. They were pitiful. He had two gallons of water and the lunch that his mother had given him. But Lancaster was determined to be optimistic. He worked out that the water could last him seven days. In that time, he was sure he would be rescued.

The long wait began. Every day, Lancaster drank his ration of water, and wrote his thoughts in the logbook. On the first night, he made flares from the fabric of the plane, soaking strips in fuel and setting them alight. He continued all night, lighting one flare every twenty minutes or so. But even though they burned brightly, no one saw them.

In the next few days, he wondered whether to set out on foot to find help, but knew that he would probably die all the more quickly this way. From the air, a man walking in the desert is almost invisible; at least, if rescuers flew overhead, they would see the plane. "*I must stick to the ship,*" he wrote.

It was a terrible place to have crashed, right in the heart of the Sahara. The dunes spread out in all directions. The daytime heat was scorching, and Lancaster wore only his underwear as he tried to conserve his energy in the shade. But the nights were bitterly cold, and he wore everything he had to stay warm enough. "*Truly am I atoning for any wrong done on this earth. I do not want to die. I want desperately to live,*" he wrote.

There were few signs of any life at all. Once, he spotted a vulture circling above him, no doubt hoping for a meal. He also saw a small brown bird nearby, and wondered if it was far to an oasis. But he kept his resolve, and stayed under the wing of the plane.

By the end of the fourth day, however, his hopes of rescue were beginning to fade. "*Do not grieve,*" he wrote to his parents and Chubbie. "*I have only myself to blame for everything.*" But after writing this, his heart suddenly gave a leap of hope. There, in the darkness, was an aircraft flare! Trembling with excitement,

Lancaster lit a flare himself. "*I assume I am located,*" he wrote in the log. "*I trust so.*"

In his relief and jubilation, Lancaster drank two rations of water. He would not die after all! The next day, he watched the horizon hopefully. Not long now, he thought to himself. Not long now...

But still no one came. His hopes faded again, and he felt tortured by thirst. "*I wish I had not drunk that extra flask of water,*" he wrote regretfully. "*Oh for water, water.*" His thirst was terrible. It was driving him crazy. But, in spite of everything, he kept his dignity. In his desperate state, he began to think about death. "*Please God I pass out like a gentleman,*" he wrote. And it certainly seems as though he managed to do so.

On the seventh day, he realized he had only a few more hours to live. With the last of his strength, he wrote messages to each member of his family, assuring them of his love. "*The chin is right up to the last I hope. Am now tying this log book up in fabric...*"

With all his documents tied to the plane, Bill awaited the end. It must have taken slightly longer than he had imagined, for he found the energy to write one last message on the Shell fuel card: "*No one to blame... Goodbye, Father old man... And goodbye my darlings. Bill.*"

While Bill lay dying, the search for him was still going on. The French officials at Reggan had sent out a search car, as they had promised; but, as the plane had crashed 60km (37 miles) from the road, there was little chance of it being spotted. The airborne searches took place much further south; no one imagined that he would crash quite so soon after taking off, even in his weary condition. Eventually, the search was called off.

Those left behind had to face an agonizing question. Had Bill wanted to die? His life had certainly pushed him to the edge. As the years passed, they had to accept that they would probably never know. 29 years is a very long time to wait.

Afterwards

Chubbie Miller resigned herself to Bill's death and married a British pilot in 1936. She was still alive when the French patrol finally found the Avro Avian in 1962. They handed Bill's logbook and other documents to her.

Bill Lancaster's mummified body was buried in Reggan by the French patrol.

In 1975, an Australian team set out to rescue the remains of the Avian. They took the plane back to Australia, where it can now be seen in the Queensland Air Museum.

Into the Valley of Death

Something glistened in the waters of the river. Something small, like a pebble. But this was no ordinary pebble. James Marshall bent forward and picked it up. He examined it carefully, turning it over in the palm of his hand.

"Looks like…" he muttered under his breath, his heart thumping. "Can it be? Surely not. Can it really be gold?"

He stared around him in the waters of the river. Soon, he found another. Suppressing his excitement, he pocketed the strange pebbles to show to his boss later. It was January 24, 1848 – the most fateful day in the history of California.

Marshall and his employer, John Sutter, tested the 'pebbles' and found that they had indeed struck gold. They tried to keep it quiet. Sutter had settled in California to run a farm, not dig for gold. He didn't want to be overrun with treasure-hunters. But it was no good. Somehow, over the next year, the word trickled out – gold! Gold! There was gold to be found in the American river.

In 1849, the 'Gold Rush' began. People from all

over America began to head west to California, seeking their fortune. But getting there was a problem. Some people risked the terrible sea voyage that took them all the way around the tip of South America and up the west coast. Thousands and thousands of others packed up their wagons and headed west on foot, risking the desert and its treacherous mountains instead. Either way, the journey took months, and the suffering along the way was dreadful.

By the summer of 1849, there was a well-established trail over the Rocky Mountains to the gold fields, which became known as the Oregon Trail. Its final stretches were the most difficult – the mountains of the Sierra Nevada formed a monstrous barrier, even greater than the huge expanses of desert. With winter snows on the way, these mountains would soon become impassable.

Despite the coming winter, the flood of people over the Rockies continued. Many stopped at the Mormon town of Salt Lake City, in Utah, where there was plenty of grazing for their livestock. The Mormons advised against taking the mountain route in winter – people had been trapped in the snows the winter before. People wondered what to do, and some just settled down to wait until the spring.

But there was another option. There was a route that led south, skirting around the Sierra Nevada. It was longer than the Oregon Trail, but it was said to be easier, with no major mountains to cross. A Mormon named Captain Hunt came forward and said he could lead the way for $10 a wagon. "I'll get you to California in nine weeks," he claimed.

About 150 people took up his offer. One group was a band of 36 young men from Galesburg, Illinois, who called themselves the Jayhawkers. There were also many families with women and children – the Bennetts, the Arcanes, the Briers and the Wades, to name a few. And there were individuals, loosely grouped together or on their own. Two of these men were to play a very important role in the weeks to come. Their names were William Lewis Manly and John Rogers.

The wagon train set off, heading south. Everyone was in a great mood. The weather was beautiful and they were on the move again towards their exciting new life. But, after about ten days, Captain Hunt began to get into difficulties. He didn't seem to know the way very well after all, and the land was getting dryer. Soon it would be difficult to find water.

Discontent began to spread. There were stories of another route that went directly west. Some people remembered seeing a map of it, in Salt Lake City. They came to the conclusion that Captain Hunt didn't know what he was talking about. Why not leave him, and cut a way through west? The Jayhawkers were the most excited by this idea, and gradually others began to agree with them.

When they reached the place where the 'short-cut' was supposed to begin, Captain Hunt lost his control of the group. The Jayhawkers had too many followers. About a hundred wagons followed them, leaving Captain Hunt with only seven.

"I think the route is unsafe," Captain Hunt told them. But he wished them well, all the same. "Goodbye and good luck," he shouted, as he waved them off.

Still in good spirits, the split-off group headed west. But, after only three days, there seemed to be no easy trail for the wagons. This alarmed many people. They were running out of food, and what kind of a short-cut came to a dead end after only three days? After much discussion, more than seventy of the wagons turned back, to chase after Captain Hunt. The Jayhawkers and a straggling selection of other people stayed on, determined to forge a way west.

The remaining group was soon in serious trouble. The land grew more and more arid, and the grazing petered out. They had now reached the desert, and everyone was thirsty. As the oxen grew weaker, they couldn't pull the heavy wagons, and people began to throw their belongings away to make the loads lighter. Tools, books, furniture – they didn't matter any more. All that mattered was getting across the desert.

They were now completely, utterly lost. They had no idea how far it was to California. The desert seemed to go on forever – a terrible land, covered in the white salts and alkalis that came up from the ground. The cattle began to collapse with exhaustion, one by one. When they did so, the people killed and ate them, because they were now very short of food. The situation was looking desperate. The group began to splinter into fragments. The Jayhawkers – mainly young, fit men – forged on ahead, leaving the families behind. The Bennetts and Arcanes stuck together, joined by a few others, making a group of about 20 people. William Lewis Manly and John Rogers stayed with them, helping to scout ahead and bring whatever water they could find.

After many days of parched walking, the Jayhawkers wandered into a deep, desolate valley. Nothing grew there; it was barren, covered only in the salts that made any water foul and bitter to drink. Gradually, the other groups converged there, too, and wandered around trying to find a way out. The Bennett-Arcane group stopped at a spring where the water was drinkable. It was almost Christmas – but what a terrible, cheerless Christmas they faced. There seemed to be no way out of this desert abyss. The sheer wall of a mountain rose to the west.

The Jayhawkers made up their minds. They decided to abandon their cumbersome wagons and pack everything they could onto their oxen, and try to find a way through the mountains. A few others followed them, including the Brier family. Mrs. Brier had to leave behind her best silver tableware, because the truth was staring them in the face. They had to abandon everything – or die.

But not everyone wanted to take this risk. The Bennett-Arcane group decided it was hopeless to continue without knowing what lay ahead. Both the Bennetts and Arcanes had a young child in the family, and Mrs. Arcane was five months pregnant. What if they got stuck in the mountains without any water? They decided instead to stay by the spring, while two went on ahead to find a way through and come back with provisions. The two men chosen were William Lewis Manly and John Rogers.

"We will wait for 18 days," said Mr. Bennett. "If you're not back after that, we will assume you have died in the mountains, or that Indians have killed you."

Another ox had died, so the men packed away some dried meat for their journey. Everyone pooled their money, a total of $60, and gave it to them for provisions. Then the whole camp gathered to wish them goodbye. In their hearts, many doubted that the two men would ever return. The atmosphere was heavy, and the women stood weeping.

"God save you," muttered the men. "Good luck to you."

Manly and Rogers shook hands with everyone, solemnly. Then they turned and made their way up the canyon.

When they had gone, a desolate air settled over the camp. Everyone knew that they might be facing death in the valley. They had some meat, for now.

But, other than that, their supplies of food were very low. They put the rest of their flour aside, to feed the children.

The hours crawled by. The children cried constantly in hunger and misery. There was nothing for them to do. The valley was one of the bleakest places on earth – just bare rock and salt. It would be a terrible place to die.

Meanwhile, Manly and Rogers struggled up the mountains. Once they had reached higher ground, they tried to assess how far they would have to walk. What they found was very depressing. There was not just one mountain range to cross, but three – with long, parched desert valleys in between.

"We will never be able to return in 18 days," said Manly grimly.

As they plodded on, they came upon something lying in a ravine, roughly covered with sage brushwood. "What's that?" exclaimed Rogers. They crept closer.

"It's a body," said Manly.

It was a man's body, lying where he had finally collapsed. Manly and Rogers recognized him. His name was Mr. Fish. He had been part of a small group who had followed the Jayhawkers. The parched mountains had been too much for him, and here he was – lying deserted on the rocks.

Their hearts heavy, Manly and Rogers continued. The going was treacherous and difficult, even for strong men such as themselves. They drank the last of their water, but soon their mouths became so dry that they could not eat their ox-meat. On one day, they were lucky enough to find a piece of ice. They melted it, gulped down the water thirstily, and ate some of their meat. Refreshed, they pressed on – but they knew they would need to find more water soon, or meet the same fate as the unfortunate Mr. Fish.

As they walked, Manly suddenly stopped. "Rogers! Look," he said, pointing.

Rogers stared. "Smoke," he exclaimed. A thin plume was rising from a valley nearby. "That means people… and water."

The two men looked at each other. The fire might belong to Native Americans, who might well kill them. Could they take the risk of finding out? Their thirst decided the issue for them. Even if it meant fighting, it was worth going to see.

To their delight, they had stumbled across the Jayhawkers, who welcomed them warmly. Sitting around the fire, the weary men heard how everyone else was doing. Some people had abandoned all their cattle and gone on ahead. The Brier family were struggling on behind. But another man had died.

"His name was Isham," said the Jayhawkers. "He couldn't keep up. When we stopped to camp, we went back and took him some water. But he was too far gone, and he soon died."

Manly and Rogers were very grateful for the company, and for all the information. They thanked the Jayhawkers, and went their own way again. Time was passing, and the families would be wondering what had become of them.

Back at the camp, the passing days grew only more miserable. The group was terrified of being attacked by Native Americans, and many did not really believe that Rogers and Manly would come back for them. "No one but a fool would come back to this place to save us," they said.

Some of the individuals soon decided to try their chances on their own. "It's everyone for themselves," they said. "We're eating our cattle, but soon there won't be any food left. It's crazy to sit around waiting."

The Bennett and Arcane families watched them go, feeling desolate. It was all very well for these people, who had no children to look after; even if they were right, there was little the families could do. It was too much of a risk to take the children over the mountains. They would just have to wait.

"Are you going, too?" they asked an older man named Captain Culverwell. He hesitated, his face troubled. He didn't like to leave the families on their own, without a way to defend themselves. But there was something in what the others had said – it really was everyone for himself. There was no point in dying in the desert. He waited for a few more days, trying to make up his mind. Then he, too, said his farewells, and trudged off on his own.

18 days came and went, and still there was no sign of the rescuers. The families grew more depressed with each passing day. "They're lost," said Mrs. Bennett sadly. "I'm sure of it. They would have returned by now."

But Manly and Rogers were not lost. After almost two weeks of trekking, they had reached a ranch, and then a whole settlement. California, at last! Hurriedly, they bought provisions with the money entrusted to them, and three horses and a mule to carry everything. Then off they set once more, back across the desert.

It was easier now that they knew the way, but the horses and mule posed a new problem. How could they manage the treacherous mountain passes, which the men had only just managed to scramble through themselves?

They reached one particularly difficult canyon, and the horses stopped. They would go no further. A precipice rose in front of them, and there was no way around. Desperately frustrated, the men realized they would have to let the horses go. They removed the baggage from their backs, and released them. "They'll die here," said Manly bitterly. "There's nothing for them to eat or drink."

Having lost the horses, they were determined to save the mule. He had proved himself to be strong and brave, even though he had only one eye. They pushed and shoved and shouted until at last the mule leaped upwards, onto a precarious ledge. Another leap, and the worst was over. The two men almost cried in relief.

But a sad sight awaited them further on. Rogers, who was walking ahead, suddenly stopped and stared.

"What is it?" called Manly.

"It's Captain Culverwell," replied Rogers. "He's dead."

The two men stared down at the old man. He was lying on his back, with his empty water container beside him. The desert had claimed another victim.

It was almost a month since Manly and Rogers had set out when, finally, they walked back into the little camp. The Bennetts and Arcanes were so moved and relieved to see them that they could barely speak. They stood silently, tears streaming down their faces. Then Mrs. Bennett ran to Manly and fell down at his feet, clasping her arms around his knees. "We didn't think you'd come back," she said in a trembling voice. But once they had overcome their disbelief, the camp came alive with eagerness and chatter. Manly warned them that the road ahead was not an easy one. California was much further than they had thought. The families listened, then bravely made their preparations. They had survived this long – they would not be defeated now.

The group set off with eight oxen and the faithful little mule. After a couple of days, they had climbed up into the Panamint Mountains and could look

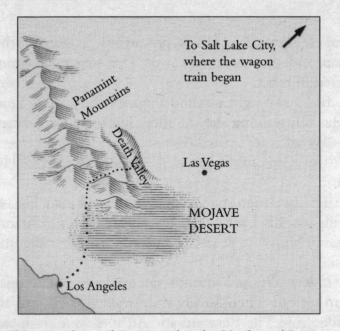

To Salt Lake City, where the wagon train began

Panamint Mountains

Death Valley

Las Vegas

MOJAVE DESERT

Los Angeles

This map shows the route taken by Manly and Rogers.

down upon the barren valley where they had almost died. It stretched out behind them, desolate and empty. Mr. Bennett shook his head, and turned away.

"Goodbye, Death Valley," he said.

The valley has been known by this name ever since.

Afterwards

Like most of the 25,000 people who headed west in the 1849 Gold Rush, few of the Death Valley survivors made their fortune in the gold fields. Many did not even work in the mines; but the flood of people created a whole new community, where many businesses were able to flourish. John Rogers worked as a carpenter and a mechanic; William Lewis Manly did a variety of jobs, including some time working in the mines. He kept in touch with many of his fellow survivors, who always viewed him as a hero, and wrote a book about their experiences, called *Death Valley in '49*.

Mrs. Arcane had her baby four months after leaving the desert, and named her Julia. Sadly, Julia died only 19 days later.

Captain Hunt succeeded in bringing the main group of wagons to California. Most of the Jayhawkers also survived, and went on to start panning for gold. A few of them had some success for a while, but they found it very hard work and the rewards were not as great as they had expected. Most of them gave up and turned to other trades, or became farmers. Some even left California and returned home.

Mrs. Brier was one of the few people to recover her possessions from Death Valley. When the gold in California began to dry up, stories began to spread of gold and silver in the desert. Prospectors began to hunt, and some of them went to Death Valley. There, Mrs Brier's silver tableware was found, untouched; and the prospectors returned it to her.

The road to Timbuktu

"The greatest traveller in the world!" At least, that's how Abu'Abdallah Ibn Battuta has been described by some historians. In the 14th century, not many men would relish the idea of crossing the Sahara Desert – let alone at the age of 49. But for Ibn Battuta, this was his final challenge before settling down to everyday life in his homeland of Morocco.

Ibn Battuta was born in Tangiers, on the north coast of Morocco, in 1304. When he was only 21, he set off on a pilgrimage to the holy city of Mecca, in Arabia. This journey is called the *hajj*, and all Muslims are expected to go on it at least once in their lifetime, if they can afford it. Little did Ibn Battuta know where his journey would take him: along the North African coast to Egypt, Palestine and Syria, before he even got to Mecca… then, before returning home, to Iraq, Persia, the east coast of Africa, Oman and the Persian Gulf, Asia Minor (modern-day Turkey), the Black Sea and Constantinople, and eventually India, via Afghanistan. From there, he journeyed to the Maldive Islands, and headed further east to China and Indonesia. When he at last returned home to Morocco, he had been exploring for 24 years.

Even by modern standards, you'd think that would be enough for anyone. But there was one place that Ibn Battuta still wanted to visit, and that was Mali, to the south of the great Sahara Desert. He had heard that it was a country of fabulous riches, one of the world's greatest sources of gold. He couldn't resist going on one last trip; so, in the autumn of 1351, he set off from the city of Fez, and headed south.

It has never been easy to cross the vast expanses of the Sahara. In the 14th century, though, there were many established trade routes across the desert, which meant that it was relatively busy. The big caravans preferred to travel in the early months of the year when the desert was not unbearably hot; so, after crossing the Atlas Mountains, Ibn Battuta settled down to wait in a town called Sijilmasa. This was on the fringes of the desert – the ideal place to buy some camels and get ready for the big journey ahead.

Despite being such an adventurer, Ibn Battuta had no plans for a heroic journey on his own. When he eventually set out across the desert, he had plenty of company. As well as his own camels, there was a whole caravan of merchants of Sijilmasa. They were all guided by a nomadic Berber tribesman, who knew the desert very well.

The caravan plodded along slowly, walking in the early morning, and resting in the heat of the day; then setting off again as the afternoon wore on. It took 25 days to reach the first settlement, a strange and desolate place called Taghaza. Nothing grew there – it existed only because of its salt mine. Ibn Battuta hated it. *"This is a village with nothing good about it,"* he wrote. *"It is the most fly-ridden of places."* The people of Taghaza had a miserable life, hauling huge blocks of salt from the mines to be carried south by camel. They relied on merchants to bring them food, because the land was so barren. But it was an interesting place, nevertheless. There was so much salt that the people built houses with it. Ibn Battuta stayed in a house with walls of salt, and a roof made of camel hide, and he worshipped in a mosque made the same way. He also noticed that there was plenty of money around. Large amounts of gold were changing hands in exchange for the salt.

Much as he was relieved to leave, he knew that the toughest part of the journey lay ahead – 800km (500 miles) of sand, with only one waterhole. But Ibn Battuta was lucky. There had been rain in the desert that winter, and the caravan found pools of water along the way, trapped in the rocks. It made the treacherous journey a lot easier. Even so, they lost one of their companions. After an argument with another member of the caravan, a man named Ibn Ziri lagged behind. He never caught up – and no one ever saw him again.

Ibn Battuta himself reached the waterhole safely, but he was worried about the rest of the trip. They were only halfway across the sands, and the desert, as far as he was concerned, was full of horrible dangers.

He worried that their guide would lose his way and that they would run out of water or get caught by the 'demons' that lived in the barren wastes. He wasn't enjoying himself much. But he needn't have worried. After a trek of about ten days, the caravan entered Walata – now in modern-day Mauritania, but at the time a provincial town of the sultanate of Mali. Ibn Battuta had safely completed yet another journey.

Ibn Battuta may have been getting grumpy after his lifetime of travel, because he complained about many of his experiences in Mali. He certainly didn't have the wonderful riches of Mali lavished upon him as he had perhaps hoped. He was very sick for two months of his stay – he ate some poorly cooked yams and nearly died – which can't have helped his impressions much. And he was thoroughly disgusted by the welcome he received. As such a seasoned explorer, he saw himself as an important diplomatic figure, and expected kings to welcome him with extravagant gifts. The Sultan of Mali gave him only a meal of bread, meat and yogurt.

Ibn Battuta was very offended. "What shall I say of you to other sultans?" he asked.

After that, the sultan was more generous, and gave him a house and later, when he left, a gift of gold.

Ibn Battuta was interested in the customs of Mali, but shocked by many of them. Mali was a Muslim country, but its customs didn't fit in with his idea of how Muslims should behave. In Walata, he was

139

horrified to discover that men and women were often friends, and could quite openly meet up with each other to chat and enjoy themselves. Ibn Battuta was used to the sexes being kept strictly apart. Later, in the capital of Mali, he was disgusted that slave girls were allowed to wander around without any clothes, and he didn't like the royal poets, either, in their flamboyant feathery costumes and masks.

But it wasn't all bad. He was fascinated to watch the sultan's lavish festivals, and he was impressed with how strictly children were taught the Koran, Islam's holy book. He explored much of the country and visited the famous city of Timbuktu before it was famous. In the 14th century, it was still a fairly small provincial town. There was little to indicate that it would become a wealthy trading post and a place where Islamic studies would flourish over the next two centuries.

From Timbuktu, he went east to Kawkaw, now known as Gao. It was the easternmost of Mali's important towns, and here Ibn Battuta decided he'd seen enough. He began to think about going home. Gao was a long way east from Walata, and he didn't want to retrace his footsteps. Instead, he planned to head north across the Sahara by a different route – north-east from Gao as far as the oasis of Takedda, then north-west back to Sijilmasa. This route would take him through some of the most inhospitable desert in the world, and this time he wouldn't have the advantage of the cool winter months. It was the

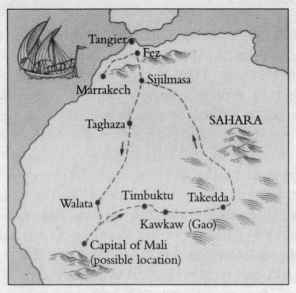

Map showing Ibn Battuta's last great trip

height of summer. Ibn Battuta clearly relied heavily on the caravans he joined, because he bought only two camels for this exhausting trek north: a male camel to ride, and a she-camel to carry his goods. It was not the best kind of planning for a summer's march across the Sahara.

The journey went badly right from the start. The poor she-camel couldn't take the heat and all her baggage, and she soon collapsed. Now the intrepid voyager was in real trouble. Fortunately, other people with the caravan offered to help him carry his provisions, sharing them out between them – or most of them did. Tempers were evidently frayed in the heat, for one man refused to help, and even refused to give water to Ibn Battuta's servant.

They now passed though the lands of some Tuareg people, desert nomads who still live in northern Mali and Mauritania. They survived partly by extorting 'protection money': caravans were obliged to take them on as guides, or risk being attacked. Despite this, Ibn Battuta was fascinated – especially by their women, who fattened themselves up with cow's milk and pounded millet. At that time, thin women were not considered beautiful (modern Tuaregs still have the same opinion), and Ibn Battuta admired these women very much. But his pleasures on the journey to Takedda were few. He became sick in the searing heat, and was greatly relieved to reach the oasis.

Takedda was a big trading post and, like Taghaza, made a great deal of its wealth from a local mine – this time a copper mine. It was not as barren as Taghaza, and the people were able to grow a little wheat. Here, Ibn Battuta found a community of fellow Moroccans to stay with and settled down for a rest. He didn't seem at all interested in continuing his exhausting journey.

But then, unexpectedly, he received orders from the Sultan of Fez to return immediately. It's not clear why, and it seems odd that the sultan should have kept such a close eye on where he was, even in the desert. But Ibn Battuta set off soon afterwards, joining a huge slave caravan of 600 black women slaves, bound for Sijilmasa. It must have been a terrible journey for them, and they had little to look forward to – they would be sold in Morocco as servants or prostitutes. But Ibn Battuta didn't give the issue a second thought; this was all perfectly normal in North Africa at the time.

On the way to Sijilmasa, the caravan encountered more nomads – this time a Berber group, who wore veils across their faces. They extorted a payment of cloth before allowing the group to continue, which annoyed Ibn Battuta very much. "There is no good in them," he complained. But this was the only major problem he encountered, apart from the constant discomfort of desert travel. After this, they passed through the Berber country in peace.

He arrived in Sijilmasa in the winter, and made a treacherous journey across the Atlas mountains in the snow. Despite his great treks across the desert, he declared that this final leg of the journey to Fez had been the most difficult of all.

Afterwards

Once back in Fez, Ibn Battuta was home for good. We don't know much about what happened to him after this – we can only assume that he settled down to a luxurious life in the sultan's court, where he would have had many tales to tell. He certainly lived long enough to write an account of his travels, known as the *Rihla* – a fascinating insight into many of the world's Muslim countries in the 14th century.

Glossary

Arabian camels *Also known as* dromedaries. One-humped camels. Originally from Arabia, but now seen across the Sahara.

Bactrian camels Two-humped camels from the Far East.

Bedouin *Also called* Beduin *or* Bedu. General name for nomadic tribes of the Middle East and part of the Sahara. There are many different tribes, each with their own name and customs.

Caravan Group of people, usually traders, making a journey together across the desert, often with a large number of camels.

Date palms Trees commonly found in the Middle East and the Sahara. A valuable source of food.

Dehydration Literally, 'losing water'. In dry conditions, especially hot deserts, people lose water very quickly by sweating, and this can be fatal.

Desert An area of land which receives less than 10cm (4 inches) of rain each year.

Desertification Process by which land that was once fertile turns into desert.

Dune A mound of windswept sand. The highest dunes in the world are in the Namib Desert (Namibia).

Erg An area of shifting sand dunes, particularly in the Sahara. Two of the biggest ergs are in Algeria – the Great Eastern Erg and the Great Western Erg.

Flash flood Sudden flood in the desert caused by rain.

Islam Main religion of people of the Sahara and Arabia. Founded in the 7th century by the prophet Mohammed, in the Arabian city of Mecca.

Mirage The illusion that you can see something up ahead when it is actually far away. Mirages are often experienced in deserts because they are caused by hot air, which refracts (bends) the light.

Mud flat Flat area of mud or clay that was once covered in water but has now dried out.

Muslim A follower of Islam.

Nomad Someone who doesn't live in one place, but moves around constantly. Most desert people are nomads because they need to travel to find water and food.

Oasis Area of naturally occurring water in a desert, usually from underground springs.

Salt flat Flat area of salt left behind by water as it evaporated.

Tuareg Nomadic tribes of the western Sahara.

Wadi Dried-up desert riverbed, which only flows if there is rain.